CLHBEC.

Leadership and Curriculum in the Primary School

LEADERSHIP AND CURRICULUM IN THE PRIMARY SCHOOL

The Roles of Senior and Middle Management

by Christopher Day, Carol Hall,
Philip Gammage and Martin Coles

P·C·P

Paul Chapman
Publishing Ltd

Copyright © 1993 Christopher Day, Carol Hall, Philip Gammage and Martin Coles

Paul Chapman Publishing Ltd
144 Liverpool Road
London
N1 1LA

British Library Cataloguing in Publication Data

Day, Christopher
    Leadership and Curriculum in the Primary
    School: Roles of Senior and Middle
    Management. – (Education Management
    Series)
    I. Title II. Series
    372.12
    ISBN 1-85396-214-7

Typeset by Inforum, Rowlands Castle, Hants
Printed in Great Britain by Athenæum Press Ltd, Gateshead, Tyne & Wear

B C D E 9 8 7 6 5

CONTENTS

NOTES ON CONTRIBUTORS

Christopher Day is Professor of Education in the Faculty of Education, University of Nottingham. He has worked as a teacher, lecturer and local authority adviser and researched and written extensively in the area of professional development. Recent publications include *Managing Primary Schools in the 1990s* (1990), (Paul Chapman Publishing) *Appraisal and Professional Development in Primary Schools* (1987) (Open University Press), and *Managing the Professional Development of Teachers* (1991) (Open University Press). He is series editor for *Developing Teachers and Teaching* (Open University Press). He is currently Head of Research and Development.

Professor Philip Gammage trained at Goldsmith's College, London and taught in London schools for almost ten years, before studying psychology and teaching at Bristol University. He has taught in the UK, Spain, Australia, USA and Canada and is now Dean of the University of Nottingham School of Education. He has published various books on education, psychology and curriculum.

He is particularly interested in Early Childhood Education and still (occasionally) teaches kindergarten-aged children. For the most part he is convinced that child-centred approaches do work, and that kicking the teacher in times of recession is no substitute for acknowledging the central importance of education for the survival of a caring society.

Carol Hall trained as a teacher and taught English and PSE in Nottingham before beginning a career in educational consultancy and writing. She has worked extensively throughout the country with LEAs,

TVEI and both primary and secondary schools on aspects of human relations training. She has written and researched in the area of human relations and management and is the co-author of *Human Relations in Education* (1988), *Scripted Fantasy in the Classroom* (1990) and *Effective Working Relationships* (in press, 1993). Currently she is one of the directors of the Centre for the Study of Human Relations in the School of Education and teaches on programmes for the School of Education as well as on the MBA in the School of Management and Finance. Her own particular areas of interest are in interpersonal skills training for managers, group dynamics and organisational effectiveness and human relations.

Martin Coles trained as a primary teacher and taught for twelve years in primary schools in England and Zambia. He was the Headteacher of a First School in Oxford before moving to Portsmouth Polytechnic where he directed the Portsmouth Philosophy for Children Project. He is now a lecturer in Education at the University of Nottingham. He has published widely in the areas of primary curriculum, children's language and the teaching of thinking.

INTRODUCTION

This book has been written from a recognition of the importance to school development and effectiveness of a much neglected 'senior and middle management' group of teachers. Whilst shelves groan under the weight of books and papers concerned with headship in primary schools, there are few which address the issues which are of direct concern to deputy heads, co-ordinators and other postholders. These teachers have an increasingly visible and central role to play not only in the implementation of the National Curriculum, pupil assessment, school development planning and associated in-service activities but also in the continuing review and development of these. Moreover, the development of the culture of the school is dependent not only upon their participation but also their leadership. Whilst initial teacher training equips teachers to 'manage' their classrooms, it does not prepare them for their roles and responsibilities in working with adult colleagues; and the in-service opportunities for leadership development and training mostly consist of learning on the job or at best short-burst 'quick fix' half-days and days. This is strange, particularly when conditions of employment for all teachers include

5 (a) Reviewing from time to time methods of teaching and pro-
        grammes of work.
   (b) Participating in arrangements for further training and pro-
        fessional development as a teacher.
6 Advising and co-operating with the Headteacher and other
   teachers (or any one or more of them) on the preparation and
   development of courses of study, teaching materials, teaching

programmes, methods of teaching and assessment and pastoral arrangements.

11 (a) Contributing to the selection for appointment and professional development of other teachers and non-teaching staff, including the induction and assessment of new and probationary teachers.
    (b) Co-ordinating or managing the work of other teachers.
    (c) Taking such part as may be required in the review, development and management of activities relating to the curriculum, organisational and pastoral functions of the school.

[DES, 1987, p5]

Much has been written about the historical development of the curriculum postholder and this has been summarised elsewhere (Campbell, 1985). Campbell summarised the activities expected of postholders as:

1 *Curriculum skills*, that is those skills and qualities involved in knowledge about the curriculum area for which the postholder has responsibility.

   (a) Knowledge of subjects. The postholder must keep up to date in her or his subject, and must know its conceptual structure and methods.
   (b) Professional skills. The postholder must draw up a programme of work, manage its implementation, maintain it and assess its effectiveness.
   (c) Professional judgement. The postholder must know about, and discriminate between, various materials and approaches in her or his subject, must relate them to children's developmental stages, manage the school's resources, and achieve a match between the curriculum and the pupils' abilities.

2 *Interpersonal skills,* that is those skills and qualities arising from the postholder's relationships with colleagues and other adults.

   (a) Social skills. The postholder must work with colleagues, leading discussion groups, teaching alongside colleagues, helping develop their confidence in his or her subject, advising probationers, etc.
   (b) External representation. The postholder must represent his

or her subject to outsiders (other teachers, advisers, governors, parents, etc).

(Campbell, 1985, p53)

Clearly the role is complex, and contains at least three sources of uncertainty:

(a) ambiguity in relationships with class teachers, an inherent mismatch between formal status and actual power derived from status.
(b) conflicting priorities (a problem of time).
(c) strain in the 'teacher as educationist' role of leading various modes of professional development work (high visibility, 'no place to hide').

(based on Campbell, 1985, p68)

The so-called WAR report (DES, 1992) advises that headteachers should have 'a vision of what their schools should become' (156), and that 'policies should emerge from collective staff discussion' (158) and 'the development of shared educational beliefs' (156). However, its authors also remind us that Headteachers 'cannot be expected to possess the subject knowledge needed . . . nor be expected to keep abreast of all relevant developments' (159). On the contrary, they should delegate, 'spell out' responsibilities and accountabilities of co-ordinators, and 'take opportunities publicly to enhance the standing of their co-ordinators by, for example, supporting or personally implementing developments recommended by co-ordinators' (159). The management of the curriculum and the leadership of colleagues cannot be divorced. Effective school development depends upon a recognition of their interdependence.

This book provides intellectual and practical support, recognising the value and enhancing the standing of co-ordinators. The titles and contents of the chapters demonstrate concern for the twin strands of their role – leadership and curriculum. Both require enabling, educative leadership which is founded upon clarity of values, knowledge of self and others, and an awareness of the complexities of leading development and change in the uncertain world of schools in the 1990s and beyond. The first three chapters in Part One focus upon the contributions that can be made by senior and middle management to school culture, teamwork, meetings, and professional development of themselves and others. Integral to the discussion of ideas in each chapter are a series of related practical activities which may be used as part of a leader's individual development programme and as leadership strategies with colleagues. The fourth chapter focuses upon assertiveness in working in different settings – a much neglected area in the management of schools' literature and the role of women as leaders.

The first three chapters in the second part of the book are concerned with curriculum matters which are of major importance to all teachers and especially those with leadership roles. They provide an international perspective upon the content–process debate, a consideration of integration within the framework of the National Curriculum, and practical suggestions for review and evaluation. In the final chapter we turn again to a consideration of the purposes of schooling, revisiting the values upon which teaching and leadership may be based – the essential moral voice of teaching.

Finally, this is not a 'tips for teachers' book. We have more respect for their professionalism than this. It is a book which will, we hope, expand horizons, present new thinking and practice. We make no apologies for this. At a time when the temptation is to react to the immediate, we hope that its contents will provide reason for reflection on past, present and future action. It is a book into which teachers should be able to dip in order to reflect on the 'what', the 'how' and the 'why' of curriculum and leadership. We hope that it will provide support and challenge, and that it will make a contribution to the thinking and practice of that very special group of colleagues whom, for want of a better term, we choose to call 'middle management'.

Christopher Day
Carol Hall
Philip Gammage
Martin Coles
School of Education
University of Nottingham

PART I
EDUCATIVE LEADERSHIP

1

DEVELOPING CURRICULUM LEADERSHIP

This chapter examines the roles and responsibilities of curriculum leaders. Whether you are a Deputy Head, area co-ordinator or postholder, as a leader you will need special qualities and skills of thinking, planning and action which enable you to work with colleagues in management roles. The chapter is divided into three parts. The first part considers ways in which the co-ordinator may work with the school culture; the second part considers the curriculum leader's needs to know herself, the job and the situation in which she works; and the final part discusses the need for a job description.

Survival, maintenance, vision

Much development work in schools over the last decade or more has been focused upon meeting the needs of schools and teachers identified as a result of externally imposed, centrally directed innovation. It has focused upon implementation of pre-ordained curriculum guidelines, conditions of service, and other legislated reforms. Teachers and schools have been forced to adapt and, whilst there have been casualties, most have survived. Three 'metaphors' of leadership were identified through a study of North American school principals (Bredeson, 1988), but apply equally to those in other school leadership roles. *Survival* is a metaphor with which all classroom teachers are familiar. It focuses upon meeting immediate needs as they arise in the classroom through short-term planning and 'present time' decision-making which takes little account of core values or long-term consequences. It is important to recognise the survival metaphor explicitly, and for it to be part of every curriculum leader's thinking, for one consequence of the predominance of the survival mind set is a loss of perspective, a temptation in some colleagues to adopt a 'siege' or 'victim' mentality, for morale and professional efficacy to slip. This should not be surprising, since for many colleagues, perhaps some readers of this book, the changes in primary education since 1988 have caused

- *Loss* of long held beliefs, established practices, habits, self confidence and self-esteem.
- *Anxiety* about being able to cope with an uncertain future requiring the acquisition and use of new knowledge and skills.
- *Struggle* to survive and adapt.

ACTIVITY 1.1

Consider any losses, anxiety and struggle which you or your colleagues are currently facing, and how this affects your area of development and leadership role.

Maintenance is a major activity for all teachers and leaders and has been defined as 'the action of continuing, carrying on, preserving' (Bredeson, 1988, p306). The act of simply maintaining the quality of organisation, teaching and opportunities for learning in the classroom is an energy consuming task. Many Deputy Heads and postholders, particularly though not exclusively in smaller schools, are full-time classroom teachers and *as* curriculum leaders need to model and be seen to model best practice in their own classrooms. Yet the responsibility for leading colleagues remains.

Maintenance is not enough. The broader leadership responsibilities of ensuring and monitoring planning, progression, continuity and 'quality

---

ACTIVITY 1.2

Review the leadership activities which you undertake over and above your classroom teaching role. List them and score each on a 1–5 personal satisfaction scale.

---

assurance' remain. There is little point in assuming the title of curriculum leader/co-ordinator if the accompanying role expectation is not fulfilled.

Vision. This metaphor is often associated with effective Headteachers. Michael Fullan, for example (1992, p31), associates the concept with 'integrity, listening skills, knowledge, values, analytic powers'. Bredeson (1988, p310) defines vision as:

> the . . . ability to holistically view the present, to reinterpret the mission of the school to all its constituents, and to use imagination and perceptual skills to think beyond accepted notions of what is practical and what is of immediate application in present situations.

Curriculum leaders, too, need vision both in relation to their own area of responsibility and its relationship to whole school development.

ACTIVITY 1.3

Substitute your own task role for 'school' in the above quotation, and then list the developments you would wish to see over the next five years.

Clearly, whilst survival and maintenance are important, development through vision is a vital part of the curriculum leader's role.

The curriculum leader as 'reflective practitioner'

The role of the curriculum leader or co-ordinator is central to the development of the school in four ways.

- *Contribution to the School Development Plan* will be a product of discussions involving the curriculum co-ordinators. Your contribution will be based upon a knowledge of:
  - (a) your area of responsibility;
  - (b) your knowledge of your area as it is being taught throughout the school;
  - (c) your knowledge of the pupils' learning;
  - (d) your vision of the future for your area.
- *Contribution to the school culture* will be, in part, a product with the way people relate to each other, and you have a significant role in the elaboration of and influence on this.

- *Contribution to educative leadership*, defined as 'helping professional educators work with others to shape their purposes and the meanings that they use to make sense of, and justify, their involvement in and contribution to education'. It is concerned with an active analysis of the way things are seen to be, and with the creation of preferred ways of doing things (Duignan and Mac-Pherson, 1992, p3)

    Being an 'educative' leader means recognising, for example, that your colleagues learn naturally, though not all in the same ways or at the same rate. Like you, they will be at different stages of their career development. It is important to recognise, for example, that some may be less enthusiastic and have less energy than you for perfectly acceptable reasons. Your 'intervention' into their learning worlds must relate to their learning contexts. Chapter Three develops this theme in more detail.

- *Reflective practice*. It is easy, particularly at times of stress caused, for example, by innovation overload often connected with the external imposition of Local Management of Schools, National Curriculum, Appraisal, Parents' Charters and the like, to place most if not all of your energies on survival and maintenance and less on 'vision'. Yet reflection in, on and about the action is important.

Understanding and working with culture

Over many years researchers and practitioners have pointed to the importance of 'climate', 'ethos', 'milieu' or 'culture' to the effectiveness of schools. We present three definitions of culture for further consideration, the first for its comprehensiveness, the second for its simplicity; and the third for its focus.

Definition 1

Culture can be described as the collective programming of the mind that distinguishes the members of one school from another. Cultural life in schools is constructed reality, and leaders play a key part in building this reality. School culture includes values, symbols, beliefs and shared meaning of parents, students, teachers and others conceived as a group or community. Culture governs what is of worth for this group and how members should think, feel and behave. The 'stuff' of culture includes a school's customs and traditions; historical accounts; stated and unstated understandings; habits, norms and expectations; common meanings and shared assumptions. The more understood, accepted and cohesive the culture of a school, the better able it is to move in concert toward ideals it holds and objectives it wishes to pursue.

(Sergiovanni and Corbally, 1984, viii)

Definition 2

Culture – another word for social reality – is both product and process, the shaper of human interaction and the outcome of it, continually created and recreated by people's ongoing interactions.

(Jelinek, Smircich and Hirsch, 1983, p336)

Definition 3

In simple terms, culture is the way we do things and relate to each other around here.

(Fullan and Hargreaves, 1992)

The first definition emphasises the complexity of school life, the need to look beneath the surface signs and symbols, and the importance of shared cultural norms if a school is to identify and work towards its objectives. The second reminds us that we *all* play an active role in shaping culture. The third affirms that whilst cultures are influenced by external factors (eg school architecture, pay and conditions of service, catchment, etc), it is the people working in the school who can and do make a difference.

School cultures are built through the day-to-day business of school life, the ways in which colleagues relate to and communicate with each other, their pupils and broader community. Cultures are born and grow. They cannot easily be superimposed. Culture is not itself visible, but is made visible only through its representation.

In a recent paper on the 'new professionalism' David Hargreaves (1992) identified signs of change in what he described as the 'dominant' and 'powerful and pervasive' culture of individualism in schools. In this culture, often mistakenly associated with professional autonomy, teachers continue 'to teach largely within the isolated privacy of their

---

ACTIVITY 1.4

What are the characteristics of your culture? Use the following headings
as 'pegs' for your thinking, and add others as appropriate against these
headings.

Relationships (Staff)
Relationships (Pupil–pupil)   Customs
Relationships (Pupil–staff)   Leadership
Values   Style(s)
Symbols
Traditions

---

own classrooms, insulated from observation and criticism, . . . are reluctant to share professional problems . . . display the same anti-intellectual
suspicion of talking seriously about education in general terms as op-
posed to gossiping about the particularities of school life . . .
(Hargreaves, 1992). He and others have noted that one of the unin-
tended consequences of recent government reforms has been the increased need for collaboration. In the new era of National Curriculum,
Local School Management, budgetary devolution, institutional development planning and increased public visibility and accountability it is no
longer possible to maintain easily cultures of individualism.

> When the pressure for change, coming simultaneously from a variety of
> sources but especially from central government, is unprecedentedly mas-
> sive in scope and scale, then withdrawal into individualism becomes both
> difficult and professionally dangerous. Few are able to exercise that com-
> bination of immunity and self-reliance that individuality requires . . .
> Externally imposed change is forcing primary teachers to rely on col-
> leagues and to co-ordinate with them to an unusual extent. Curriculum
> leaders and consultants who have acquired greater expertise in a founda-
> tion subject of the National Curriculum emerge and are treated by col-
> leagues as an expert resource for staff and pupils alike.
>
> (Hargreaves, 1992)

Whilst life for curriculum leaders may not be as positive as this may
imply – and other chapters in this book highlight difficulties in and
strategies for dealing with individual responses to imposed change –
recognition that schools and their cultures may be in a transition stage is
important, for it allows increased understanding and, with that, opportunities for appropriate leadership.

MANAGEMENT CULTURES

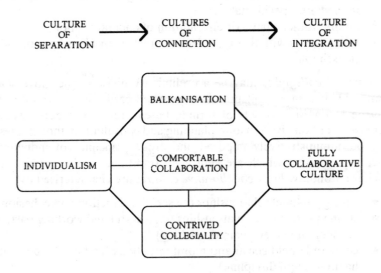

MANAGEMENT CULTURES

Figure 1.1 School cultures, adapted from Fullan and Hargreaves (1992)

Figure 1.1 presents examples of five management cultures identified by Fullan and Hargreaves (1992). We have characterised these as cultures of separation, connection and integration. The characteristics of the individualism culture have already been described. In this school there is a sense of professional isolation, habitual patterns of working alone, no feedback to teachers on their effectiveness from outside the classroom, safe, non-risk taking forms of teaching. In the three 'cultures of connection', *Balkanisation* is characterised by:

- separate and competing groups whose first loyalty is to the group and its beliefs rather than those of the school, where these are different;
- squabbles over resources and territory;
- poor continuity and expectations of pupils.

Comfortable collaboration is characterised by:

- high participation in decision-making;
- warmth, camaraderie on personal not professional levels;
- reactive not proactive planning;
- collaboration at the level of advice-giving, materials sharing of an immediate, specific nature;
- an oral rather than written tradition of communication;
- little contact with theory, reflective practice, or ideas from outside the school.

Contrived collegiality may be a preliminary phase in the movement from individualism to collaboration described earlier in this chapter. It may be recognised by sets of formal, bureaucratic procedures which increase attention given to joint planning and consultation, though these may be administratively imposed and erode principles of individual teacher judgement which are central to traditional understandings of teacher autonomy. *Fully collaborative cultures* are characterised by:

- strong personal relationships (eg social interaction and cohesion);
- strong professional relationships (eg task-related working parties, curriculum leaders, paired teaching);
- commonly held social and moral intentions (eg beliefs about behaviour, pupil discipline);
- agreed curricular intentions (eg curriculum policy statements);
- failure and uncertainty are not protected or defended, but shared and discussed with a view to gaining help and support;
- the individual and the group are simultaneously and inherently valued (Nias, Southworth and Campbell, 1992).

ACTIVITY 1.5

Reconsider your responses to the previous activity. Which of the elements in your lists most readily relate to the cultures described above?

It is unlikely that the types of culture described will always match reality. It is more likely that each is on its own continuum. That is, there will be 'strong' and 'weak' forms of each. Schools may well possess some characteristics of, for example, 'comfortable collaboration', and others of 'fully collaborative' cultures. Judith Warren Little in research into school improvement in North America in the early 1980s, described some of the benefits of collegial approaches to planning and development.

> Instead of grasping for the single dramatic event or the special achievements of a few children as the main source of pride, teachers (enjoying conditions of collegiality) are more able to detect and celebrate a pattern of accomplishments within and across classrooms.
>
> (Little, 1987, p497)

Yet she was also able to observe weak and 'strong' versions of collegiality.

Know yourself: reflective practice

One philosopher of education (Hodgkinson, 1983) identified four maxims which are fundamental to effective leadership:

- Know the task
- Know the situation
- Know the followership
- Know thyself

In this part we look more closely at knowing self and the situation. We assume that all those reading this book will already have good knowledge of their teaching area. Knowing the followership is the focus for Chapter Three.

When Hodgkinson writes about self-knowledge, he is in effect concerned with the importance for leaders to develop 'personal professional knowledge'; and this involves processes of reflecting upon the events of one's practice (Carter, 1992, p118). If we are to grow, we *must* take account of the relationship between values, actions and consequences. If we do not recognise this in ourselves, how will we recognise it in others? 'Reflective practitioner' is a term coined by Donald Schon (1983) in a book of the same name. He is concerned in his writing about the nature of professional effectiveness; and, with others, recognises the need to use *reflection* as a means of learning. As always the question of time is raised. When, in a busy day filled with 'doing' does any class teacher, let alone one with additional responsibilities, find time to reflect? What is involved in the process of reflection anyway? And why is it so important – what are the benefits to be derived? Let's try to take it step by step.

First, there is the question of the job itself – teaching. What does it involve? Well, certainly it is value laden (Chapter Eight). It is not a neutral activity. It involves selection (of content, purposes, methods). The question, however, not only concerns what we do and how we do it, but also what messages we are giving. What values are we transmitting, communicating to our pupils, our colleagues in school, the parents of our pupils, and the wider community by what we do? In a sense, the answer lies in the culture which is communicated through such channels as the physical environment, the school 'norms', 'rules', expectations, symbols and ceremonies, and the way we relate to each other. However, how much are we aware of this on a personal level?

Much of our behaviour and the motivations, purposes and values which underpin it is at an intuitive, implicit level. When was the last time you asked yourself why you spoke to pupils (or a pupil) in the way you did yesterday, or why you choose to approach your planning in a particular way?

There is a sense in which the predominating classroom culture of 'busyness' is a function of the need to survive rather than the need to educate (Sharp and Green, 1974). So if we are to check our effectiveness, 'how we are doing' as teachers, it will be necessary to find ways of getting feedback both from self and colleagues about ourselves, both as teachers and as leaders.

The purpose of reflection is to expose implicit values, assumptions, planning and behaviour to analysis.

> Through reflection it is possible to reconstruct, to re-build a narrative that 'remakes' the taken-for-granted, habitual ways we all have of responding to curriculum situations.
>
> (Connelly and Clandinin, 1988)

Donald Schon describes *reflection-in-action* which takes place in the midst of action itself, usually at an almost subconscious level as we strive to respond and initiate in living situations. This, Schon claims (1992), results in *'knowing-in-action'* ie the knowing built into and revealed by our performance of everyday routines in action. Much of this is tacit. He contrasts this with *'reflection-on-action'* and *reflection on knowing in action* which occur outside the immediate teaching situation, are more contemplative, and often use a mental 'action replay' mode. He calls this 'thought turned back on itself'. Others have added to these two kinds of reflection another – *reflection-about-action* – in which we not only reflect on the action itself but also the social and political situation in which it occurred in order to understand or 'know' it more fully. It is easy to fit these abstract notions of reflection into, for example, a five-level model of reflective practice.

• reflection-in-action	1.	rapid reaction (instinctive, immediate).
	2.	repair (habitual, pause for thought, fast, on the spot).
• reflection-on-action	3.	review (time out to re-assess, over hours or days).
	4.	research (systematic, sharply focused, over weeks or months).
• reflection-about-action	5.	re-theorise and re-formulate (abstract, rigorous, clearly formulated, over months or years).

(adapted from Griffiths and Tann, 1991)

We do not suggest that all of these should occur simultaneously. There will be a 'felt need' link with phases of personal and professional development described in Chapter Three. However, it is easy to see that if reflection on practice whilst in the midst of practice is the only kind used, then professional growth will be limited and, ultimately, limiting to teaching effectiveness.

Promoting reflective practice: roles and relationships

> Teachers placed in positions that bear the titles and resources of leadership display a caution towards their colleagues that is both poignant and eminently sensible. The relation with other teachers that is implied by terms like mentor, adviser or specialist has little place in the ordinary workings of most schools. Even the simple etiquette of teacher leadership is unclear.
>
> (Little, 1988, p84)

The important principle of being an 'educative' curriculum leader is that our primary purpose is to help others 'shape their purposes and the meanings that they use to make sense of, and to justify, their involvement in and contribution to education' (Duignan and Macpherson, 1992, p3). This is based upon the belief that colleagues learn best through the provision of a supportive climate, environment and kinds of 'critical friendship' support from colleagues which respect their autonomy and build upon their experience. This is not to say, however, that support should not be accompanied by challenge!

Evers et al (in Duignan and Macpherson, 1992, p20) present five criteria against which educative leaders should be judged:

- their ability to develop and maintain an effective enquiry and problem-solving culture in their domain;
- their respect and tolerance of different points of view and an acceptance of criticism as the key ingredient in the growth of knowledge in the organisation;
- their ability to adapt to challenges and provide for change in policy or practices through participative feedback and reflection;
- their concern to ensure that people have the freedom to fully participate in this process of learning and growth;
- their commitment to the holistic belief that their decisions can be defended on the basis of their contribution to the benefits of long-term learning within the organisation.

(Evers, 1992)

Whilst this is written in the context of action research into school leadership generally, it nevertheless applies to all in leadership roles. For the curriculum leader, key words are 'respect', 'adapt to challenges', 'tolerance', 'participative feedback', 'problem-solving' and 'contribution to long-term learning'.

The curriculum leader must:

- Be an enthusiastic model.
- Acknowledge participants' concerns.
- Focus on the positive, building on strengths.
- Celebrate risk-taking and challenge.
- Generate support from influential people.
- Be adaptive, so that she may, as appropriate, be a catalyst, a resource helper, a (learning) process helper, a consultant, a solution giver.
- Be close to rather than distant from colleagues.

The consultancy process is one which is predicated upon a human relationship characterised by mutual emotional and intellectual involvement. So relationships are clearly the key to success in leading staff development. It is not merely knowing self and knowing the task, but *knowing your colleagues* and achieving their respect which is vital. To foster and maintain relationships requires considerable commitment and expertise by all concerned, particuarly in the face of the kinds of resistance to change which will be described in Chapter 3. The curriculum leader must be able to work with colleagues in identifying needs, motivate (self and others), plan, negotiate, and evaluate. She must be skilled in self-reflection and leading others in this.

ACTIVITY 1.6

Plot your relationships with colleagues on a 'close'–'distant' axis. Placing yourself in the centre, draw lines out to different colleagues. The length of line indicates the closeness or distance of the professional relationship. When you have done this, consider the reasons for this.

(close colleague)

SELF ———————————————— (distant colleague)

You will probably have identified some teachers who spend their careers in relative isolation from others in their profession, who are, therefore, apprehensive about change, and may be defensive and protective of their present teaching. Such teachers lack a risk-taking, growth-oriented process approach. The curriculum leader who is concerned with staff development must recognise this and, whilst not losing sight of the need to promote change and a recognition that conflict is an inherent part of the change process, must *acknowledge* colleagues' concerns, fears and anxieties. Many years ago, Ronald Havelock (1973, p12) wrote that 'the first task of a change agent is to establish contact and build a relationship with the people he wants to help'. Research on staff development indicates two basic ingredients for success – a supportive environment and well-planned activities which are responsive to need and involve teachers at all stages to encourage ownership. It should include:

- *Theory* in order to extend current knowledge about the underlying principles of content, teaching or roles.
- *Modelling* so that the curriculum leader or in-service event leader, by her actions, models the values and practices which she is presenting as best practice.

- *Demonstration* ways of enacting ideas in practice.
- *Practice* opportunities for staff to 'try things out'.
- *Feedback* by the leader and/or colleagues on practice.
- *Peer coaching* continuing support of colleagues through peer observation and other support.

In order to achieve these key activities curriculum leaders need:

- Knowledge of colleagues' needs.
- Knowledge of the relationship between these and organisational needs.
- Acceptance by colleagues.
- Ability to listen to, negotiate and 'contract' with colleagues.
- Ability to plan, implement and evaluate in-service events and other forms of staff development.
- Ability to provide ongoing support.

All of these imply the need to form and maintain 'partnership' relationships over time. Whilst all of these relationships will be underpinned by care and respect for colleagues, the ways in which they are enacted will differ according to individual need.

The curriculum leader must work with colleagues as an equal. There is no 'automatic right to lead' such as that implied by the title of, for example, Head or Deputy. Hargreaves (1990) identifies two orientations in working relationships which are useful to a discussion of the curriculum teacher's role.

- *Implementation* This is characterised 'by an emphasis on the achievement of short-term, predictable goals and on discharging defined duties in specific tasks and events'.
- *Development* This is aimed at 'less predictable, long-term change and the opening up of new learning opportunities through sustained enquiry'.

The distinctions between the nature and context of the two kinds of partnerships may be summarised as shown in Figure 1.2.

Clearly, these orientations are not mutually exclusive. There are times when it is entirely appropriate for the curriculum leader to be involved in an implementation relationship, for example, in planning staff development days or other short in-service events. In the longer term, however, it is development partnerships which are likely to provide the firm foundations for growth.

Development partnerships	Implementation partnerships
Voluntary	Imposed
Informal/spontaneous	Formal/planned
Sustained/evolving	Brief events
Organic	Mechanistic
Responsive	Discharging of specified duties
Low prediction	High prediction

(Biott, 1991, p11)

Figure 1.2 The two kinds of partnership

Curriculum leader as consultant

It is clear that the curriculum leader must act as *process* rather than *task* expert in developing partnerships. In writing about experiential approaches to organisational development, Harvey and Brown (1988) identify five styles of consultancy which are useful to the curriculum leader's thinking:

- The *agreeable* style. This indicates an 'underdog', or slightly subservient, role in which you avoid controversy.
- The *supportive* style. This encourages closeness of relationships, emphasising colleagues' strengths, avoiding confrontation, and building trust through respect.
- The *analytical* style. Here you are able to apply your expertise or experience through rational discussion of a problem identified by a colleague.
- The *persuasive* style. This supports and influences colleagues. It is non-confrontational and is often an attempt to forge compromise between individual and organisational goals.
- The *integrative* style. This is the most challenging, for it attempts through collaborative work to develop a shared participatory learning culture. It is characterised by team building.

(Harvey and Brown, 1988)

ACTIVITY 1.7

It is likely that you will have used each of these styles in working with colleagues, according to circumstance and your own preferred way of working. Identify which of these styles you use the most. How may you extend your repertoire?

Critical friends and contracting

Working in a leadership role as an equal among equals can be a lonely business, and it is important to consider opportunities for teaching and learning with colleagues. One such opportunity is by the establishment of critical friendships.

These have been defined as 'practical partnerships entered into voluntarily, based on a relationship between equals and rooted in a common task or shared concern . . . critical friendships can serve to decrease isolation'. (Day, Whitaker and Johnston, 1990)

Clearly, it is important to become a friend before becoming a critic. Essentially the role of a critical friend (or 'key colleague') is to provide *support and challenge*.

What is the nature of the relationship between critical friends?

Colleagues talk to one another about teaching, often at a level of detail that makes their exchange both theoretically rich and practically meaningful . . . It illuminates underlying principles and ideas in a way that allows teachers to understand and accommodate one another, to assist one another and sometimes to challenge one another.
(Little, 1987)

What roles may a critical friend play?
You will find that at different times you will be an enabler, a coach, a counsellor, a challenger (of ideas, opinion) a catalyst, or just someone to talk with!

How do I begin?
You may decide to begin just by talking things through.

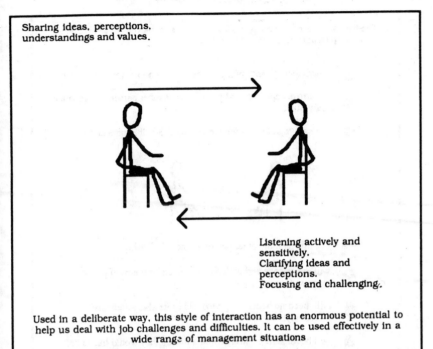

Sharing ideas, perceptions, understandings and values.

Listening actively and sensitively. Clarifying ideas and perceptions. Focusing and challenging.

Used in a deliberate way, this style of interaction has an enormous potential to help us deal with job challenges and difficulties. It can be used effectively in a wide range of management situations

Figure 1.3   The critical friendship process

How does it work in practice?

Essentially, every critical friendship that works is one in which both colleagues help each other within a relationship which is both person- and task-centred.

It may be informal or formal, but always there should be an expectation that both colleagues will gain from the friendship both professionally (conversations will be designed to enhance reflection upon practice) and personally (conversations will be designed to encourage the growth of self esteem).

Do we need to agree ground rules in advance?

Sometimes, it can be helpful to consider forming an agreement or contract: the helping process needs to be 'owned' by both critical friends and there needs to be some basic understanding as to the major goals to

"The true benefits of a helping relationship can be achieved if I can create a relationship characterized on my part by:

- a genuineness and transparency, in which I am my real feelings;

- a warm acceptance, and prizing of the other person as a separate individual;

- a sensitive ability to see the world as the other person sees it.

If I can achieve this then the other person in the relationship :

- will experience and understand aspects of themself previously repressed;

- will become better integrated and more able to function effectively;

- will become more similar to the person they would like to be;

- will become more self directing and self confident;

- will become more of a person, more unique and more self expressive;

- will be more understanding, more accepting of others;

- will be able to cope with the problems of life more adequately and more comfortably."

Figure 1.4 The helping relationship

be pursued and procedures to be used in the helping process so they both own the same thing.

An explicit contract, whether verbal *or* written, between critical friends can help achieve these goals. The contract need not be too detailed or too rigid. It needs to provide structure for the relationship and the work to be done without being frightening or overwhelming. Written or at least explicit verbal contracts can do much to clarify mutual expectations about ways of working and goals, but inflexibility and irrevocable commitment to initial goals need to be avoided. Instead you need to build in times for review of progress (of task and relationship) at regular intervals.

In summary:

- The contract should be negotiated, not imposed, by the parties involved.
- The contract should be clear to all involved parties. They should know what 'helping' is about.
- Some kind of oral or written commitment to the contract should be obtained.
- The contract should be reviewed as the parties progress and revised if necessary.

(Based on Egan, 1982)

Job descriptions

Finally, all teachers in the school will have an agreed job description which is regularly reviewed. It is hard to envisage how any curriculum leader could exist without this as a reference point for her work. Here is advice offered by the National Association of Headteachers to its members:

1   The nature and purpose of job descriptions

1.1   A job description is a description of an individual teacher's professional duties, responsibilities and status within the school. It will inform staff within the school of the teacher's responsibilities, and to whom/for whom the teacher is responsible. A job description should be clear and informative, not long and complex.

1.2   A job description will provide a current statement of what is expected of a particular teacher, Deputy or Headteacher. It therefore has contractual implications, in that failure by a teacher to carry out a duty listed in the job description would be breach of contract. The job description should reflect the full range of a teacher's responsibilities, inside the classroom and out, and should be subject to review and modification on a regular basis following consultation between teacher and Head.

1.3   Job descriptions are crucial to the appraisal process; teacher, Deputy Head and Head appraisal should be based on a current job description. It may well also provide the opportunity to consider changes to the appraisee's job description.

1.4   Job descriptions should be public documents within a school, so that all staff are aware of where responsibility for areas of school organisation or activities lies. Such openness will not be achieved easily or quickly in all schools, and there will be a need for the staff to be consulted on the context and propriety of publication of job descriptions within school.

1.5   It is important to distinguish between a *job description* and a *job specification*. The *former* is concerned with the agreed professional role of a teacher within school following discussion of individual and institutional needs. The *latter* is a statement of requirements for a post and is more to do with recruitment and selection. It could be issued to applicants for a post, listing requirements for that post and identifying criteria which will be used in making an appointment.

2   Teachers' job descriptions

2.1   Each job description will need to contain:

2.1.1   Common headings to identify the school, name of post holder, job title, the person to whom the teacher is responsible and the date from which the job description becomes effective.

2.1.2   A short statement about the teacher's general duties. A good example might be:

The education and welfare of a designated class/group of pupils in accordance with the requirements of Conditions of Employment of School Teachers, having due regard to the requirements of the National Curriculum, the school's aims, objectives and schemes of work, and any policies of the Governing Body. To share in the corporate responsibility for the well being and discipline of all pupils.

Those drawing up job descriptions would need to ensure that the wording of any such statement was appropriate to the needs of the school.

2.1.3   Definition of specific responsibilities of the post held, such as:

to manage a departmental budget of [. . .] established in consultation with senior staff and governors.

Responsibility for Science throughout the lower school.

Contribute to the general management of the school as a member of the Senior Management Team.

2.1.4   Specific tasks/objectives, as agreed from time to time. Some tasks might well be temporary, either because they will be completed by a certain date or because it is envisaged that someone else will take on the responsibility in the future. Such parameters need to be clarified.

2.1.5   A date at which review of the job description is planned.

2.1.6   A statement that it may be amended at any time after consultation with the teacher.

(NAHT, 1992)

Job descriptions should be written in simple but clear terms, should not be over-prescriptive, and should reflect priorities within the School Development Plan. They should evolve from consultation, and allow scope for personal and professional development.

ACTIVITY 1.8

- Do you have a job description which is available to colleagues?
- Who was involved in writing it?
- Is it regularly reviewed?
- How does it relate to the School Development Plan?
- Review your job description. Does it match with your personal and professional development needs?
- If it does not, or you do not have one, talk it over with your head or deputy.

2

MAKING PEOPLE A PRIORITY

A leader is best
When people barely know that he exists,
Not so good when people obey and acclaim him,
Worst when they despise him . . .
But of a good leader, who talks little,
When his work is done, his aim fulfilled,
They will all say, 'We did this ourselves'.

Lao-tse

In this chapter we set out to define the key components of enabling curriculum leadership by Heads, Deputies and postholders, as we understand them. These components are viewed in terms of interpersonal qualities and values as well as the structural and organisational framework necessary to carry out curriculum development in primary schools. We will discuss why schools need enabling leaders and will examine some of the emotional blocks to effective curriculum leadership and suggest ways of overcoming them. These include examining blocks which both women and men teachers experience to becoming fully enabling leaders as well as understanding how the dynamics of even the best intentioned teams can sabotage innovative or effective strategic curriculum planning and implementation.

In the beginning: taking on a leadership role

Every primary classroom teacher reading this chapter knows in his or her heart what being a leader means. They know it because they live it, every working day of their lives. They are the functional experts on leadership in the classroom and feel themselves to be comfortable in this domain. Their professional training was built around the development of skills and approaches to the management of learning in the classroom; but it is the struggle to become a leader of children in a classroom that is often most vividly recalled from college days. From our own experience of teaching practice, we can all summon up a memory of the stomach-wrenching fear that being left 'in charge' for the first time in a classroom produced; through the first tentative experiments in creative lesson planning and relationship building, to a more mature understanding of how best to encourage, support and challenge children in their primary task – learning. The confidence that we win for ourselves as leaders in the classroom is fought long and hard for and yet strangely, as we may discover, this skill of leadership is not instantly transferable or generalisable to other situations outside the classroom. In fact the staffroom, just a few doors down the corridor, may in itself come to represent an enormous psychological barrier if we are invited to take on a leadership responsibility with colleagues.

For whether you are a Head, Deputy or postholder, becoming a curriculum leader demands that you draw upon resources, inner and outer, that may have been neglected or remained unchallenged for some time. The view that we have of ourselves as competent teachers will be derived mainly from our work with children not necessarily from working with our colleagues. Despite the exhortations of management experts, working with other teachers on curriculum development is often perceived as secondary to the most important task of *getting on with the job* – teaching in the classroom. Indeed teachers report job satisfaction as deriving most significantly from working with children not with other teachers. The intrinsic reward and the joy of the profession for many lies in seeing children blossom under careful tutelage. It is not uncommon to hear teachers say, 'I love the kids, it's the teachers I can't stand'.

Basic teacher self-esteem needs are met through the quality of these productive relationships with children. We see ourselves as having some

h and purpose in our lives if we can contribute to the develop-
children in positive ways. But it is this very same need, to
maintain a sense of ourselves as worthy and worthwhile human beings
which may lead us to resist the role of curriculum leader and disable us
from taking up the role in a confident, mature way. For keeping up to
date with developments in the National Curriculum, assiduously recording SATs scores or extending a specialist knowledge base, or organising
an INSET day do not automatically equip anyone for the role of curriculum leader.

Am I up to it? Self-doubt and questioning personal competence

Even those teachers who actively seek to extend their responsibilities in
school may find that on being appointed to a curriculum development
role, the same, familiar, stomach-wrenching fear experienced as a novice
on teaching practice comes flooding back. It may result in a temporary
questioning of ability and suitability for leadership, throwing up all manner of doubts and insecurities that formerly have rarely been allowed to
surface. The title 'curriculum leader' is experienced as discomforting
and often ends up renegotiated as 'co-ordinator', which sounds far less
threatening and authoritative.

Working in a leadership role with colleagues requires us to start learning again about what it means to encourage, support, challenge and
consolidate – but this time with our peers and it will almost certainly
lead to an initial questioning of our competence to do the job. This loss
of confidence may be fleeting or longer lasting. Certainly this loss of
confidence will mean a temporary blow to our self-esteem. Expressions
of support from colleagues at this stage, although reassuring, are not by
themselves sufficient to take away that period of initial doubt and uncertainty brought about by the question, 'Am I capable of taking on this
responsibility?'

This is a crucial growth point for the leadership process and for the
enabling leader. The temptation to deny these feelings on the one hand
or to permit them to overwhelm on the other is equally damaging. If you
allow yourself to fall into either of these traps, it will be difficult in the
future to support colleagues constructively who no doubt will also fall
victim to this type of negative self-talk at some time.

What you can do

- *articulate* your feelings of doubt or insecurity with someone you trust to listen empathically.
- *accept* that taking on a challenge requires a period of uncertainty.
- *argue* the need for clear boundaries and responsibilities with the Headteacher.
- *act* giving yourself permission not to be the perfect leader.

Remember:

- You know what leadership is, you do it every day.
- You are used to leading children.
- You will have less experience leading adults.
- Expect that being given the title curriculum leader (or similar) will lead to an initial period of self-doubt and questioning of competence. This will pass.
- You can do it if you equip yourself with the tools.
- Growth and development are only achieved through challenge and struggle.
- You will have to be prepared to learn.
- You are a member of a team not *the* team.
- You will need to struggle intellectually and critically with your understanding of the role. Talk to colleagues about what their expectations of leadership entail.
- Be prepared to offer a definition of your role and its functions as you understand them with the curriculum team.

Understanding enabling leadership

We will argue that enabling leadership is an interactive process which is evidenced in groups, teams or communities where there is a common, shared purpose which is understood and owned by all members. The management of the school is best understood as synonymous with the leadership of the school. Duigan (1989, in Riches and Morgan, eds.) argues that

> The maintenance of a distinction between leadership and management functions at the conceptual and or practical level is counterproductive, . . . functions, structures and processes are the systematic public organisational expression of leadership.

It is not just a trait or magical quality that is invested in one leader and dooms the rest to the role of perpetual follower or subordinate. Leadership is contextual and its definition the product of shared meanings and cultural norms. Leadership functions may be temporary as in the case of working groups or task teams or allied to a specific role as in the case of Headteacher. The opportunity to exercise leadership is both the right and responsibility of all professional teachers. It is not something which can be opted out of or left to others. Enabling leadership involves actively sharing leader functions in a systematic, coherent managed framework. It demands of each staff member self-awareness, a capacity for personal reflection, courage and a genuine, principled commitment to discover how it is possible to move forwards together in the pursuit of organisational excellence. Personal and professional authority exercised through ethical and principled action is the individual taking full responsibility for leadership within a school community. Carl Rogers (1968) predicted over 20 years ago that different models of leadership in organisations were going to be necessary to optimise efficiency in an era of accelerated change, scarce resources and increased complexity of information and technology. Though perhaps even he could not have foreseen the landslide of paper to hit primary schools since 1988!

> The only road to true efficiency seems to be that of persons communicating freely with persons – from below to above, from peer to peer, from above to below, from a member of one division to a member of another division. It is only through this elaborate, individually initiated network of open human communication that the essential information and know-how can pervade the organisation.
>
> (Rogers, 1968)

Enabling leadership is transformational. It is visionary. It is the creation of a management culture which encourages the expression of the ideal vision through the repeated and rigorous scrutiny of values. It is the intersection of individual and societal values as they are experienced by the major stakeholders in the entire school community. The interpretation and concretisation of this dialogue finds expression in the *mission statement* or *development plan* of the school. Enabling leadership seems an oddly paradoxical notion because it is simultaneously tough and tender. Tough because the personal and professional demands that individuals must make of themselves and others are of the highest ethical and moral standards and tender because to enable each other to achieve such standards means trusting, respecting, forgiving and ultimately believing in the human capacity for commitment and dedication.

Characteristics of the enabling leader

The research clearly shows that the effective leader must be *both* a 'human relations specialist' and a 'task specialist'.

(Gordon, 1980)

Gordon (1980) directs us to an awareness of the synthesis of leader functions but Schon's (1987) telling phrase, 'professional artistry', helps us to understand the demanding nature of a leadership role. For there is undoubtedly some magic in working with a collection of individuals, all of whom have their hobby horses, their likes and dislikes, their causes and their politics and transforming them into a purposeful and productive working team. It is something other than appealing to mere rationality or common sense, 'We've got to do it because the DFE say we've got to do it', that translates that ego-centred energy into an energy which enables teachers to transcend their own self-interest for the sake of the team or the school's organisational goals. 'We are doing this because we believe that this is the best way possible for us to achieve excellence in our classrooms.'

Enabling leaders not only encourage, they demand that teachers make the fullest contribution to the development of the school in its pursuit of excellence that it is possible to make. Anything else results in second best for pupils. Enabling leaders self-consciously bring to the act of management the highest standards of human integrity, responsibility, justice, equality, discipline and love. Further, they also have an unfailing belief that this is a requirement of all members of the school community, not just those with designated leader functions. Tom Peters (1989) exhorts us all to 'set absurdly high standards for integrity – and then live them, with no fuzzy margins'.

A prime task of curriculum leaders then must be to stimulate individual and staff initiatives in creative thinking and learning. This entails helping colleagues to see themselves as having the ability to contribute effectively to curriculum development and the confidence to carry it forward. Peters and Waterman (1988) in their illuminating study of America's best-run companies, *In Search of Excellence*, maintain that an overriding characteristic of what they termed 'transforming leadership' was the ability of leaders to 'obtain extraordinary effort from ordinary human beings'.

More significant, both for society and the companies, these institutions create environments in which people can blossom, develop self-esteem, and otherwise be excited participants in the business and society as a whole.

(Peters and Waterman, 1988, p86)

The profile of the enabling leader which we present here is something more than the rational, intelligent, methodical manager who moves the meeting swiftly from aims and objectives to implementation and evaluation. It is a person who is able to create and communicate an enduring vision of what is possible and desirable. To engender excitement in the translation of that vision into a reality and to nurture the belief that all members of the team have a vital role to play in the maintenance of the quality of what is produced.

Here we set out in detail the characteristics of the enabling leader. Enabling leaders are people in pursuit of excellence, in all aspects of their lives. We would guess that it would be a rare creature indeed though, who in reflecting upon the following questions, found themselves to be in possession of all the answers.

ACTIVITY 2.1

Ask yourself the following questions:

Self-awareness and personal growth
'Do I have a commitment to personal development through self-reflection and readiness for change?
Do I possess the self-discipline to realise my potential to the full?

Criticality
Have I a critical awareness of the cultural and political issues which surround curriculum planning both locally and nationally?
Am I self-questioning?

Experience
Am I willing to learn from failure or mistakes?
Do I accept responsibility for my own life?
Can I present myself as I really am?

Values
Do I have an understanding of the values which sustain my work?
Am I principle-centred in my actions?
Do people see me as a person of integrity?

Commitment
Can I be a conscious actor in the creation of a culture which sustains colleague commitment to curriculum development?
Can I motivate others to excel?
Do I believe we can do better than we are doing right now?

Do I want our school to offer pupils and parents the very best educational experience?

Do I want children's lives to be touched by what they learn in the classroom?

Do I want teachers' lives to be enriched by what they teach in classrooms?

Simplicity
Do I wish to help simplify management structures and eliminate unnecessary bureaucracy?

Resource
Can I be an information gatherer for others?

Am I willing to spend time learning, not pretending that I am the expert?

Am I a real listener?

Autonomy
Do I want to devolve power through the creation and sustenance of self-managing curriculum teams?

Do I trust people to make good decisions without me?

Facilitation
Am I capable of supporting, mentoring, mediating, problem-solving through appropriate use of counselling skills?

Do I really want to know how people feel or do I just pretend?

Mission
Do I envision curriculum development as part of a set of plans or strategies which is integrated into the school's major organisational goals?

Do I understand what it is we are trying to create?

Boundary
Do I understand where the boundaries of the role of curriculum leader lie?

Am I clear about what is my responsibility and what is not?

Do I understand my function as a boundary or gate keeper for the curriculum team?

Am I clear about the differences in responsibility between the member and leader role?

Esteem
Can I help to enhance the self-esteem of colleagues through creating a climate of high trust, respect and team ownership of problems, outcomes and successes?

Barriers to becoming an enabling leader

There are many real and sometimes seemingly impenetrable barriers to becoming an enabling leader. These exist at both the institutional and the psychological levels and need to be identified in order that they can be struggled with and in some way resolved. We would not presume to consider this an exhaustive list but in conversations with teachers over many years these features commonly re-emerge as being among the most difficult personal barriers to overcome.

Familiarity or intimacy

The challenge facing the newly appointed middle manager resides as much in persuading other colleagues of her ability to take up the role as a belief in her own competence. The group dynamics of an organisation are powerful enough to undermine even the strongest individual's perception of herself and in the minutiae of everyday interaction self-esteem can be systematically eroded by a prevailing atmosphere of cynicism, sneering and lack of respect for feelings.

Primary schools are generally tight-knit communities. We work with the same group of colleagues day in day out for months often years. We may even socialise with them outside school. Pupils live locally and parents are encouraged to access teachers in their classrooms whenever they wish to discuss matters relating to their child's schooling. Many teachers find themselves in the additional role of listening ear to parents who need to talk through the effects of marital disputes, financial worries or family traumas. What primary schools seek to evoke is an atmosphere of familiarity, or an easy, unthreatening intimacy, rather like that experienced by members of an extended family.

However, there is an emotional cost to this familiarity. Teachers themselves may often have worked together for many years and there is a feeling that people 'know' each other well. Colleagues may even feel that they have an intimate knowledge of each other's foibles, preferences and peccadilloes. Even to the extent that it becomes possible to predict with a high degree of accuracy (sometimes the exact phrase) the line an individual will take up on a given topic. One of the authors worked in a school where teachers would place bets on the reactions of certain members of staff to suggestions made by the senior management team in staff meetings.

The staffroom becomes a space for giving vent to stored up feelings, for airing frustrations or grievances and forming alliances. This expression of feelings compounds the sense of shared experiences, and helps to create a group history or mythology. Often staff will reminisce about ex-colleagues and repeat stories, usually apocryphal, about their eccentricities. Such intimacy is double-edged. On the one hand it can be comforting to feel part of a group with a shared history or that colleagues experience similar feelings of vulnerability, helplessness or incompetence but on the other hand, it can become claustrophobic, emotionally suffocating, feeling trapped into old patterns of behaviour and relationships that may be inhibiting of personal development or change. Somehow in this physical and emotional proximity, we lose the capacity, or the confidence, to surprise or be surprised. It is possible to lose sight of each other's individuality and uniqueness. No doubt we have all had the depressing experience of having been on a really involving and exciting INSET course and on return to school full of enthusiasm for a new approach only to be greeted with, 'We tried that before you came and it didn't work then' or, 'You can tell you've been on a course. You'll be trying to hold my hand next and asking me to "share"!'

Even the physical body becomes public property as clothes, shape, hair colour, weight, style are all considered areas open to discussion and critical dissection. One of us even experienced a male colleague receiving a spontaneous burst of applause when he arrived in the staffroom one day wearing a new jacket.

Robert Carkhuff (1983) writing about families suggests that they can be divided into two rough categories, retarding or facilitating. We would suggest that this is a helpful way of understanding the potential effects, both positive and negative, of familiarity or intimacy amongst a group of staff. The retarding staff culture will use familiarity, what it knows or thinks it knows about each other to undermine or disable through the erosion of self-confidence. For the curriculum leader this may take the form of being prevented from taking up aspects of the leader role appropriately.

> Sorry I had to miss the meeting last night. I had to rush into town and get my mother a birthday present. You know what she is like if I forget. I knew you wouldn't mind. Did I miss anything?

or

> Is it really necessary for us to have all these meetings? I thought that I could count on you of all people to get through the business quickly and leave us alone to get on with the job.

and

> Odd, really, the Head giving you the job. I thought he never really liked you. Stan is absolutely fed up with you because he was convinced the Head was going to ask him. You know he specialised in National Curriculum maths for his M.Ed.?

Such a set of expectations and covert demands are designed to minimise the effectiveness of the curriculum leader by a subtle appeal to friendship or collegiality. The *intention* may not be to sabotage authority consciously but for the unassertive or inexperienced leader this will inevitably be the *result*. However, failure to take up the proper responsibility and authority of the role can produce chaos and distrust, as well as the blurring of organisational boundaries, as people inevitably move in to fill the gap created by the abdication of leader responsibility.

> Do you want me to tell Sally she has got to make more of an effort to get to our meetings?

> I know I said I didn't like meetings but it's been so long since you called the last one that the group has lost all its enthusiasm. Do you want me to rally people?

> I can see you're not confident about the maths side of it. Leave it to me.

Usurping the role can result in either frustration and anger or infantilisation and feelings of helplessness.

ACTIVITY 2.2

Make your own list of similar situations when familiarity has undermined your ability to carry out your role effectively. Note down how you felt and how you responded at the time. Devise an alternative *assertive* response, that is, where you are able to communicate how you feel about the situation without putting the other person down.

A facilitating staff culture doesn't make assumptions or guesses about the feelings or responses of its members. It takes care to foster each other's sense of themselves as extraordinary people with a unique contribution to make. This is a culture which frustrates stereotypes and pigeon-holes for people and encourages self-expression. In fact it is a mirror of the classroom climate that primary school teachers seek to create in their classrooms in order to bring out the very best in their pupils.

ACTIVITY 2.3

Look critically at the assumptions you make about colleagues.
It might be helpful to choose three colleagues and for each one make a list of the assumptions you make about each of them. Are they based on fact, experience, fantasy or sheer guess work?
How might you go about checking the validity of these assumptions?
In conversation with them, try to avoid making assumptions about their responses. Really listen to what is being said. Let them surprise you.

Discussing the undiscussable – dealing with difficult colleagues

Some of us are lucky enough to work with fellow teachers we like, admire and respect for their commitment and dedication to doing a difficult job well under immensely trying circumstances. Others of us may find that we have a mixture of feelings towards colleagues but generally they are positive. However, our experience of working with teachers for many years on human relations courses leads us to believe that there is another category. That of people we not only positively *dislike* but actually find very difficult to work with indeed.

The reasons for this dislike will be legion and probably originate back in the mists of time. For the curriculum leader and the curriculum team when such strong negative feelings exist between team members, the implications for the integrity of curriculum planning can be serious. Such negativity can become a crucial dynamic if it is allowed to interfere with the work of the team. What is apparent if this situation exists is that it is often not even alluded to or discussed, except in private, where of course everyone will be aware of it. In the team or planning group, people will studiedly pretend that it is just not happening. This collusion to suppress the expression of bad feeling or even admit the possibility of bad feeling between members can and does result in an impoverished or compromised set of proposals or plans being brought forward. The unspoken criteria for their formulation may be based on the need of members to save themselves from embarrassing emotional confrontations, rather than on a real needs analysis of the pupils or the school.

Chris Argyris (1989) reports his findings from an executive development programme concerned to improve the performance of strategic planners and their teams in organisations. From conversation and observation, he discovered that the strategic plans formulated by the managers were based on four fundamental but unspoken rules of behaviour, completely unrelated to the formulation of the best possible strategic plan for their organisation.

1. Bypass embarrassment and threat whenever possible.
2. Act as though you are not bypassing them.
3. Don't discuss steps 1 and 2 while they are happening.
4. Don't discuss the undiscussability of the undiscussable.

Argyris found that by helping the managers to look at ways of confronting these difficult interpersonal relationships, coupled with a structure to facilitate the expression of difficult and potentially embarrassing opinions safely, managers felt a greater freedom to be more open and honest with each other. What we can learn from Argyris's work is quite simple. Pretending that relationships between team members do not contribute to the effectiveness or ineffectiveness of the team is at best a recipe for mediocrity and at worst an educational mishmash unrelated to needs or values. Curriculum leaders need to be aware that part of their role is to enable team members, not necessarily to like each other better, but to confront the relationship issues which may be impeding the adoption of the optimal curriculum development strategy. Chapter Four, dealing with assertiveness for curriculum leaders, spells out in some detail strategies for enabling greater openness and honesty between team members.

Carl Rogers' (1962) core conditions for helping relationships, genuineness, positive regard (respect) and empathy serve as a base line to operate from in all social interaction if we wish to nurture healthy, open relationships. We would want to add that the task of the curriculum leader must be to foster her own willingness to reframe the very notion of 'difficult people'. Difficulties and differences between people are the product of a relationship within a specific and defined context: two or more individuals being part of a difficult relationship. The concomitant of this position is that in thinking through ways to improve the relationship, you begin by accepting that you have some responsibility in it and for improving it. In short, you are at least 50 per cent of the problem!

This is not a recipe for making difficulties disappear but it is one way of facing up in a mature way to the responsibilities that professionals have to ensure that they treat each other with the respect, good manners and dignity that are the hall marks of adult behaviour.

ACTIVITY 2.4

Think of a colleague at work you are experiencing some relationship diffi-culty with right now. Note down the situation as *you* experience or feel it. Next, note down how you guess the difficult person feels about that same situation.
Try owning some responsibility for the creation of the difficulty between you. What belongs to you and what belongs to the other person?
Apply Rogers' core conditions to the situation. Are you treating this per-son with respect even if you disagree with their views? (Positive regard.)
Are you being open and honest about how you feel in the situation? (Genuineness.)
Do you have a full grasp of the other person's feelings about the situa-tion? (Empathy.)

Implications of leadership for women

Central to the discussion of curriculum leadership in the primary school must be a basic recognition of the fact that primary schools are in the main staffed by women and led by men. So that Acker (1983, cited in Reid and Stratta, 1989) found that in 'junior with infant' schools, women are 74 per cent of the teachers but only 26 per cent of the Heads. In 'junior without infant' schools they are 65 per cent of the teachers but only 16 per cent of the Heads. Women's chances for promotion are also less than men's. The National Union of Teachers and the Equal Oppor-tunities Commission reported (Riches and Morgan (eds) 1985) that pro-motion chances for women drastically *fell* between 1963 and 1983. Significantly, it was also found that 82 per cent of the sample were hoping for promotion during the course of their careers. It might be safe to assume, on the basis of this sample, that there must be appreciable numbers of women teachers in primary schools who are disappointed or frustrated in the progression of their chosen career.

Interestingly, little recognition of the effects these simple but reveal-ing statistics might engender seems to have been given in the literature on educational management. As Gray (Reid and Stratta (eds) 1989) comments pithily

> There has been no significant discussion in educational writing of the implications of gender considerations in the study of schools as organisations.

(p38)

Masculine	*Feminine*
acts as leader	affectionate
aggressive	cheerful
ambitious	childlike
analytical	compassionate
assertive	does not use harsh language
athletic	eager to soothe hurt feelings
competitive	feminine
defends own beliefs	flatterable
dominant	gentle
forceful	gullible
has leadership abilities	loves children
independent	loyal
individualistic	sensitive to the needs of others
makes decisions easily	shy
masculine	soft spoken
self-reliant	sympathetic
self-sufficient	tender
strong personality	understanding
willing to take a stand	warm
willing to take risks	yielding

Bem Sex Role Inventory, reproduced from Nelson-Jones (1986) p27.

There have been powerful and revealing studies of the effects of gender role stereotyping on school pupils and achievement but little corresponding research on the effects of discrimination at staffroom level on organisational effectiveness. Gender, then, is by no means peripheral to our discussion of enabling leadership in primary schools, still dominated numerically by women teachers but hierarchically by men. This recurrent image of the 'normalcy' or 'naturalness' of male leadership represents a potent cultural myth and one which is still enormously difficult to shift. Reid and Stratta's (1989) illuminating work, *Sex Differences in Britain*, describes the extent of the male domination of the professions at the highest levels and is prescribed reading for the sceptical.

ACTIVITY 2.5

Make a map of the pattern of distribution of role and responsibility in your school on the basis of gender for teaching and non-teaching staff. Is the patterning and distribution of power similar to or different from the figures quoted above?

The pattern of inequality, replicated throughout our social structures, becomes inextricably interwoven with our own sense of ourselves, our lived and felt gender identity. Leadership then may be a particularly difficult attribute for women to integrate as part of their sense of self-identity. This is not to say that women are not leaders or do not lead but that they do not *see* or *feel* themselves to be leaders as it finds common cultural expression in our institutions. We list (p. 38) characteristics most commonly (or stereotypically) associated with gender and it quickly becomes apparent that masculine traits, and therefore traits more likely *believed* to be attributes of men rather than women, are the ones which are associated with leadership and that feminine traits, held by women in the popular imagination, with nurturing.

Clearly there is nothing wrong per se with these clusters of attributes. What is plainly fallacious is the allocation of such attributes on the basis of gender alone. At the rational level teachers, men and women, accept that both are equally well equipped to take up a leadership role. What women actually report is that their experience is quite another (Marshall, 1990). Bayes and Newton (1985, in Colman and Geller, eds.) offer a sociopsychological interpretation of some of the emotional constraints that men and women experience when confronted with a woman in a leadership role.

> We suggest that because of the fantasy and fear of women's power, both men and women are socialised to accept a strongly held stereotype of women as possessing legitimate authority only to nurture. Therefore a woman is likely to have difficulty exercising authority in those areas that are seen as inappropriate to her sex role, and for which she receives little or no early training: maintenance of a group's external boundary, mobilisation of aggression in the service of work, establishment of a No. 2 position with her as No. 1. She is also likely to stimulate and collude in the maintenance of dependency in her staff.

If we agree with Bayes and Newton's analysis it becomes apparent that much more has to be done than paying lip-service to equal opportunities in school staffrooms. Not only will women need to counteract strong social forces in themselves and their colleagues but they have to be prepared to work towards a redefinition of what constitutes the endeavour of leadership. We believe that enabling leadership is a model which draws upon qualities and attributes construed as masculine and feminine in equal measure and that women and men will have to struggle emotionally and intellectually to redefine the role as they understand it.

ACTIVITY 2.6

What women can do
- Learn to become more assertive in relationships. Don't apologise for expressing feelings.
- Express your own needs for help or support.
- Avoid taking responsibility for the emotional caretaking in the work team.
- Learn to trust your instincts and to go with your hunches.
- Maintain a crystal clarity about the aims and purposes of the group. Maintain a balance between keeping members of the team on task and resolving relationship issues which may be preventing this.
- Articulate clearly what you want from others in meetings.
- Don't allow yourself to be sidetracked by expectations of your behaviour by others. You do not have to meet other people's expectations.
- Learn how to deal for yourself with symbolic projections about female role stereotyping, eg mother.
- Maintain awareness of the external boundaries of the group. Keep other colleagues informed, get feedback on ideas and so on.
- Don't use your sexuality to get your own way.

ACTIVITY 2.7

What men can do
- Don't fall into the trap of feeling that men *should* be leaders and that as a man you *shouldn't* feel anxious or vulnerable in the leader role.
- Be aware of ways in which people wish you to take responsibility for them.
- Be aware of ways in which you take responsibility for others.
- Allow yourself to express feelings, not act them out. If you are angry say you feel angry don't just sound angry.
- Avoid being over-controlling, of yourself and others. Allow people to say what they want to say.
- Avoid over-rationalisation and simplification. In teams the human relations dimension needs as much care, thought and nurturing as completion of the task.
- Keep in mind that men and women have different speech habits and these differences need to be respected and attended to.
- Don't use your sexuality to get your own way.

Conclusion

In this chapter we have developed the notion of enabling leadership as part of a school culture which prizes individual and team development, integrity, commitment and excellence above survival, mediocrity and compromise. In order to pursue these goals schools require individuals who are capable of maintaining the highest levels of interpersonal functioning and the ability to retain the capacity to learn in an environment where the information flow is increasing in complexity daily. This is no small challenge and there may be powerful psychological and institutional barriers to overcome. But it is a challenge which, if taken up, yields the very highest rewards in meeting the needs we all have as human beings for making a contribution towards the quality of life and learning for all members of the school community.

3

LEADING CHANGE THROUGH STAFF DEVELOPMENT

Leading change through staff development involves forming and maintaining partnerships with colleagues of different ages, experiences and interests. Partnerships which work are based upon mutual interest, respect and knowledge. Staff development is not simply a rational activity which results from an identification of need, a plan for action, action, review/ evaluation and further development which is based upon this. Of course, rational planning of this kind is necessary, but there are a number of other human factors which will contribute positively or negatively to staff development. The chapter considers how postholders may influence colleagues, and in doing so develop their teacher as educationist role relationships. Our first assumption is that it is the informal one-to-one and small group activities which form the core of leadership work, and although we present structures for planning more formal INSET work, we do so in this context. Our second assumption is that a major problem for most postholders is the provision of time outside their own classroom duties to develop their role. Most have little 'non-contact' time and rely on 'personal time', outside working hours, to plan and read, and 'snatched time' during breaks and after school (perhaps in directed time) to influence colleagues (Campbell, 1985, p161–2). This chapter focuses upon individual learning factors, the management of change, and the crucial role of the curriculum leader's relationships with colleagues.

Individual learning needs

Earlier chapters have considered the whole school culture, the context in which staff development takes place and the enabling nature of leadership. There are also what we will call *individual learning cultures* which are fashioned by individual biography and experiences of staff development. Together, these will affect the attitudes of colleagues towards staff development:

> Evidence from studies of teachers' professional life cycles illustrates important changes in teachers' concerns, relationships with pupils, and relationships with colleagues that suggested differentiated learning interests and processes throughout their careers.
>
> (Butt et al, 1992, p54.)

Unless teachers have a meaningful commitment to their own professional development and the needs of the school as a whole, no significant change will occur. So the curriculum leader who initiates staff development activity will need to think about *how* to involve colleagues, *why* INSET is needed, *what* should be done and *when* it should happen.

> nothing is of value to us unless it can enter our experience in such a way which enables us to realise what is valuable in it.
>
> (Dearden, 1968, p38)

This statement is reinforced by other educational philosophers. Carl Rogers (1969), for example, argues that only experiences that involve the learner's genuine self result in any learning of lasting significance; and John Dewey (1963) saw the values, abstractions and interests of individuals other than the learner as a potential source of distortion if they obstructed individual learners in making sense of their world (Butt et al, 1992, p58).

Job and career development

If personal and professional development is to be effective, stages of career and life cycle development must be taken into account by individuals who are responsible for their own learning and the managers who are responsible for providing support for this, whether it focuses upon personal (non-vocational), individual professional, professional as practitioner or institutional needs.

Bolam (1990) suggests five stages of job development:

1. Preparatory stage (when they wish to apply for a new job).

2. Appointment stage (when they are selected or rejected).
3. Induction stage (first two years in post).
4. In-service stage (3–5, 6–10, 11+ years in post).
5. Transitional stage (promotion, redeployment).

Leithwood (1990) offers a developmental outline of professional expertise:

1. Developing survival skills. (Knowledge about and limited skill in use of several teaching models.)
2. Becoming competent in the basic skills of instruction. (Well-developed skill in use of several teaching models.)
3. Expanding one's instructional flexibility. (Growing awareness of the need for and existence of other teaching models, efforts to expand teaching repertoire.)
4. Acquiring teaching expertise. (Skill in application of a broad repertoire of teaching models – professional plateau.)
5. Contributing to the growth of colleagues' instructional expertise. (Reflective about non-competence and beliefs/values. Able to assist others.)
6. Participating in a broad range of educational decisions at all levels. (Informed, committed to school improvement, accepts responsibility, able to exercise leadership.)

He also suggests the following career cycle development:

1. Launching the career ('reality shock'): easy or/ and painful.
2. Stabilising: developing mature commitment, feeling at ease.
3. New challenges and concerns: diversifying, seeking added responsibilities, build an alternative career.
4. Reaching a professional plateau: re-appraisal, sense of mortality, stops striving for promotion and enjoys, or stagnates, becomes cynical.
5. Preparing for retirement: focusing (positive or defensive), disenchantment, serenity.

For many teachers, INSET or staff development has consisted of a 'smorgasbord' of activities, often concerned with meeting the apparently urgent needs of classroom teaching but failing to meet the real needs of classroom and teaching development either because they were too short, poorly targeted or characterised by '101 ideas for Monday morning' – useful perhaps early in one's career, but even then of limited value since they do not address the thinking needs of teachers.

One project designed to discover the match between the learning needs of primary school teachers and the design of in-service events reported that the majority of staff development activities available to teachers were one-day or evening events. It was clear from teachers' interviews that there was no intrinsic difference between the effectiveness of on- and off-site activities; and that teachers used similar criteria for judging both. Successful activities, it seemed, met teachers' expectations for:

- *Process needs:* courses presented a balance of activities, involved working with colleagues, sharing experience, were well structured.
- *Targeting needs:* activities were focused upon needs specific to the particular age range taught (ie relevant).
- *Content needs:* courses increased knowledge/awareness, reinforcing and reassuring current thinking but encouraging participants to see issues from different perspectives.
- *Utilisation needs:* courses provided direct curriculum development benefits and application to classroom practice.
- *Leadership/modelling needs:* activities were led by tutors who were well prepared, enthusiastic, caring and aware of group dynamics.
- *Time and energy needs:* courses were timed for when energy levels were high.

However, it became clear that there were more complex learning needs which these short staff development opportunities did not meet, but which were perceived as being essential to long term growth. Teachers spoke of the planned learning experiences which had been most significant for their development. One teacher wrote of the learning which resulted from attendance at a two-year part-time Diploma course:

> It challenged my attitudes and ideas subtly over two years . . . My practice used to be very product-based, but now I can understand the child's work more and value it for what it is.

Another spoke of an extended 20-day course which had been:

> the start of my professional development . . . that opened my eyes. I learned to look outside the classroom, at how things were affecting the work inside the classroom . . . management . . . and how the staff develop as a staff.

In addition to the needs met by short-burst activities, these longer, more reflective and analytical, in-depth learning opportunities had served to improve self-esteem. Critical friendship needs were also met – in-depth opportunities for sharing knowledge and skills over time in a supportive environment.

Participants had been enabled to relate their experience of practice to theory, to reconsider critically their assumptions, predispositions, values (the why as well as the how and what of teaching), and the contexts in which they taught. They were able to develop new skills over time.

Concentration of effort on short professional learning opportunities which predominantly focus upon institutionally defined needs may well, in the long term, result in cultural isolation and parochialism (Day, 1991).

Teachers learn naturally, over time, usually out of a sense of professional need (to be more effective at their jobs), sometimes in order to acquire new knowledge and skills associated directly with the implementation of curriculum innovation; and, particularly in the early stages of their careers, in order to survive in the classroom! Their *rate of learning* (or learning curve) will be greater or less depending on these and other autobiographical and personal factors. The key messages for those involved in leading staff development, therefore, are:

- Most teachers' learning occurs naturally and usually in the privacy of their classroom or outside the school.
- Teachers, like children, cannot be developed. They can only be provided with opportunities for development. The learner's role in the learning is a crucial planning consideration for staff development leaders.
- The in-service/staff development leader is an *interventionist* in colleagues' learning lives.
- The quality of intervention and opportunities provided are paramount to the effectiveness of staff development.

Figure 3.1, 'Developing professional learning', provides a more detailed way of viewing teacher learning which takes account of the learner, the environment and variables within this.

Difficulties in leading staff development

The organisational life cycle

The complexities of leading staff development may be compounded not only by individual colleagues' learning stages and the relationship

DEVELOPING PROFESSIONAL LEARNING

Professional Learning Assumptions	Contextual Variables	Intervention (Challenge and Support)
Teachers and schools are motivated to learn by the identification of a problem or issue which concerns their professional role. This may be externally generated or arise from classroom or career needs.	The organisational culture. Self-awareness of individual. The individual learning culture.	Teachers should be offered the means to reflect as an essential part of enquiry into their thinking and practice and identification of problems and issues.
Effective learning occurs in response to reflection on and confrontation of past and present values and practices.	Provision of enabling relationships and mechanisms.	Teachers should be offered a range of high quality professional development opportunities off- and on-site through which they can begin to engage in systematic enquiry on practice which involves making theory (tacit knowledge) explicit.
Teachers have the capacity to be reflective, but not necessarily self-confrontational.	Conditions of service and/or leadership which do not encourage different levels of reflection.	Teachers should be offered affective and appropriate moral and critical support in processes of internalisation rather than identification or compliance. This support should be provided by key colleagues, so allowing teachers themselves to maintain and enhance autonomy.
Teachers' learning is organic and natural. Development (growth) precedes change (planned action).	Efficacy of need identification procedures. Skilfulness of intervention strategies. Leadership.	Teachers should be offered appropriate support in developing strategies for planning, negotiating and implementing work on their own and others' schools.
Transformation in thinking and practice is a necessary part of a teacher's developing learning process.	Individual career, life and organisational growth stages and influences which form critical 'points of departure'.	Teachers should be supported in the testing or validation of their critical theories through the provision of internal and external learning support (consultancy, networks, brokerage).

Figure 3.1   Developing professional learning

ACTIVITY 3.1

Where could you place yourself and your school in relation to these factors?

---

difficulties identified in Chapter Two, but also the organisational life cycle. The school in which you work may itself be in a period of stabilisation, reorganisation or crisis! Figure 3.2 provides one example of an organisational life cycle.

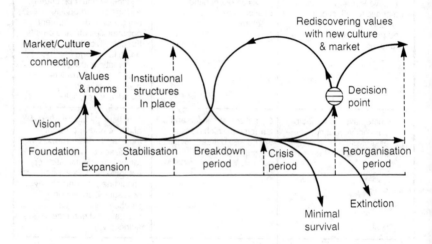

Figure 3.2   The organisational life cycle, from Hall (1992)

The *foundation* period is characterised by the strong and clear vision of the leader which 'connects with the needs of the times' and has the support of the teachers. The *expansion* period is a time when the vision is being implemented. It is characterised by a heightened sense of commitment by staff. Syllabi are written, plans drawn up. The *stabilisation* period marks an emphasis on unity and loyalty of staff who are secure in the knowledge that the school is successful and a sense of professional achievement. The *breakdown* period marks a period of crisis when existing (often long held) values and practices are questioned as a result of 'a natural alteration in society and cultural values and needs that change with time and history'. One consequence may be a loss of self-esteem, and professional institutional loyalty. It is quickly followed by the *critical* period. Should the school adopt only a survival strategy (for example, a minimalist approach to the implementation of externally imposed change) or try to 'renew' itself? The critical factor here is the ability, skill and vision of leadership, and their tolerance of the uncertainties and ambiguities which characterise this period. Finally, there is the *re-organisation* period. For this to occur, the leadership has to 're-examine its founding values, articulate them, and redefine them so that they . . . are in line with the present values and needs of society' (Hall, 1992, p22).

Whilst it is the responsibility of the Headteacher to ensure that school development planning includes a comprehensive review of 'where we've been' and 'where we are going', each curriculum leader must also have a clear sense of the particular stage in the life cycle of the organisation, for this will be the backcloth against which staff development will take place.

ACTIVITY 3.2

1. Identify the stage of organisational development your school has reached.
2. List the factors which provide evidence of this in terms of:
    (a) your own attitude to staff development.
    (b) the attitudes of colleagues.

An essential part of the renewal process itself is to support the Head and others in promoting and sustaining vision. Patrick Duignan (1987) identifies four 'critical success' norms for staff development:

1. *Collegiality*. There must be a climate of trust and openness in which professional colleagues feel comfortable in working closely with each other. Such a caring work environment encourages teachers, especially, to plan and work together to improve their teaching.

2. *Experimentation*. Teachers, especially, must be encouraged to reflect on their practice and experiment with new ways of teaching. Educational leaders must help create the conditions in which such experimentation can occur without the feeling that mistakes

will be 'frowned upon' or punished. Mistakes must be regarded as opportunities for further learning. Leaders must protect those who are educationally entrepreneurial and recognise and support those who are achieving – students and teachers.

3. *Involvement.* Structures must be shaped so that those affected by decisions are involved in making them. The rhetoric of participative and democratic decision-making is everywhere but many in schools (students, teachers, parents) still feel disenfranchised and powerless. Why does it take us so long to translate the rhetoric into reality? Why do so many people in our schools still feel that they are on the periphery, when it comes to meaningful decision-making? Even many school principals feel that they no longer play an important role in making important decisions that affect their school's life (Duignan, et al, 1984).

4. *High expectations.* One of the central findings of the effective schools literature is that effective schools have a norm of high expectations for all who participate in school life. There are high expectations for students (academic performance, discipline, citizenry etc), for teachers (quality teaching) and for leaders (to help generate a vision and get the commitment of all in the school to the vision).

The essential words and phrases within these for curriculum leaders are:

- a climate of trust and openness;
- plan and work together to improve teaching;
- reflect on practice and experiment with new ways of teaching (without the feeling that mistakes will be frowned upon);
- those affected by decisions should be involved in making them;
- high expectations for teachers (quality teaching).

These provide the basis for thinking about and planning staff development. However, they do not go far enough, for the skilled curriculum leader must also consider individual staff's stages of development and the kinds of professional learning opportunities which may be best matched to these.

We have written elsewhere of the central role of reflection in the learning process. There is also a need for *continuity.* In thinking about staff development, the curriculum leader needs to consider two factors – the individual's stage of professional and career development, and the *kinds* of planned learning opportunities which might be appropriate.

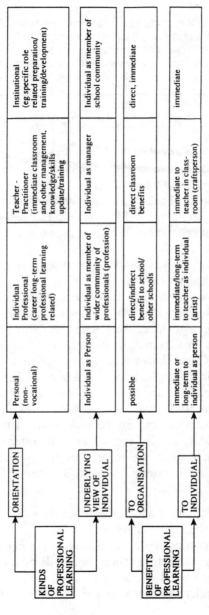

	Personal (non-vocational)	Individual Professional (career long-term professional learning related)	Teacher-Practitioner (immediate classroom and other management, knowledge/skills update/training)	Institutional (eg specific role related preparation/training/development)
ORIENTATION				
UNDERLYING VIEW OF INDIVIDUAL	Individual as Person	Individual as member of wider community of professionals (profession)	Individual as manager	Individual as member of school community
TO ORGANISATION	possible	direct/indirect benefit to school/ other schools	direct classroom benefits	direct, immediate
TO INDIVIDUAL	immediate or long-term to individual as person	immediate/long-term to teacher as individual (artist)	immediate to teacher in class-room (craftsperson)	immediate

(Left-hand labels: KINDS OF PROFESSIONAL LEARNING → ORIENTATION; BENEFITS OF PROFESSIONAL LEARNING → UNDERLYING VIEW OF INDIVIDUAL, TO ORGANISATION, TO INDIVIDUAL)

Figure 3.3   Kinds and benefits of planned learning opportunities

---

ACTIVITY 3.3

As part of the whole-school staff development plan, it is important to provide a *balance* of in-service experiences for staff. These will relate both to individual and organisationally defined needs. Use Figure 3.3 as the basis for a discussion about 'balance in professional development' with your colleagues either at a senior management team or staff meeting.

Planning the INSET day

From time to time, curriculum leaders will wish to take the opportunity provided by one of the five 'staff development' days to promote her area of responsibility. We have already emphasised the importance of 'contracting' with individual colleagues and presented success criteria identified by teachers attending INSET outside the school. Both of these provide important criteria for the planning of more formal school-based INSET events.

Needless to say, the focus for the day should be perceived as contributing to individual teacher and/or whole school development. Ideally, then, it should have evolved through staff discussion and may be part of the annual School Development Plan. The purposes should be clear, the intended outcomes stated, and the teaching–learning processes described. Figure 3.4 shows an example of one way of 'checking out' the use of different methods of teaching which are appropriate to different purposes.

It is worth noting, also, the importance of providing favourable conditions for learning. Time and timing are important 'climate setters' as is the physical environment in which the event is held, the commitment to the emotional, practical and intellectual needs of colleagues and the quality of leadership. Finally, *evaluation* is still often seen as something which is added on to staff development. On the contrary, it is an intrinsic part of the planning. Fenstermacher and Berliner (1985, p281–314) suggest that INSET should be judged for the

- *Intrinsic worth* of the focus/content area.
- *Success* in the achievement of
  - communicating objectives clearly; providing quality teaching;
  - ensuring a match between the needs of the learners and the nature of what was provided;
  - applicability (transfer to practice) of the learning.

Leading Change through Staff Development

Training Method/ Component \ Level of impact	A. General awareness of new skills	B. Organised knowledge of underlying concepts and theory	C. Learning of new skills	D. Application on-the-job
1. Presentation/ description (eg lecture) of new skills	✓	✓	✓	✓
2. Modelling the new skills (eg live or video demonstrations)		✓	✓	✓
3. Practice in simulated settings			✓	✓
4. Feedback on performance in simulated or real settings			✓	✓
5. Coaching/ assistance on the job				✓

Figure 3.4 Learning new teaching skills, Joyce and Showers (1988)

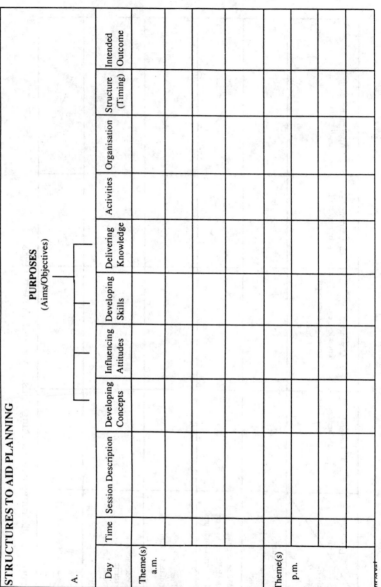

Figure 3.5 A simple structure for planning the day, session by session

- *Merit* in terms of
  - –sensibility (in use of time and talent);
  - –variability (the longevity of the use of the learning);
  - –incentive (the 'pay off' for the teacher);
  - –maintenance (the support available to sustain the learning).

These three criteria provide a useful framework for the design of simple but appropriate evaluation pro-forma, particularly when used in conjunction with the information from the planning documentation.

Within each session will last one or more learning episodes. Figure 3.6 provides a structure for thinking about learning processes which take account of adult learning needs.

Managing change

The change process

Change can involve the loss of firmly held beliefs and ideas, of comfortable habits, of established patterns of behaviours and of confidence and self-esteem. It often causes anxiety about different skills that may be required, about being able to cope, about what the future will be like. Change involves struggle to survive intact, to acquire new competences, to gain respect and recognition. Colleagues may well dislike upheaval and have a preference for the familiar, first learned techniques. It should not be surprising, therefore, if some resistance to new ideas, ways of working is encountered, particularly if new practices, beliefs, values and intentions differ from their own.

> There is a hard core in this school, and in most schools I've known, who are just 9–5 teachers. They don't want to change what they do. In a curriculum development programme it's the teachers who don't need to change who take part in it, and the ones who do need to change who never attend.
>
> (from Campbell, 1985, p72)

Whilst at least five days of in-service have become mandatory since this was written, it is still possible for colleagues to be present in body but not in spirit.

Change threatens the stability of the daily thinking and activities of teachers. It is not comfortable. It is potentially disruptive to what Huberman (1983, pp482–3 in Fullan and Stiegelbauer, 1991, p33) calls the 'classroom press' which causes teachers:

Characteristic	Implications
1 Episodic, not continuous	• Rely on short bursts of learning activity. • Break material into manageable units; but hook each one on to other items of learning.
2 Problem-centred, not curriculum-oriented; immediate goals based on needs and intentions; concrete situation; immediate, not future application	• Make relevant to students' needs for motivation. • Be aware of students' intentions. • Students to set goals. • Start where they are, not necessarily at the beginning. • Do activity now, not prepare for it in the future.
3 Learning styles:	• Be aware of different learning styles; build up learning skills.
• analogical thinking; use of existing knowledge and experience	• Relate new material to existing experience and knowledge. • Be sensitive to range and use of experience.
• trial and error	• Discovery learning; students to be active, not passive recipients. • Need for reinforcement; build in feedback. • Need for practice.
• meaningful wholes	• Move from simplified wholes to more complex wholes. • Help students to build up units to create whole; select out essential units from non-essential.
• less memory; but imitation	• Rely on understanding for retention, not memory. • Use of demonstration.
4 Lack of interest in general principles	• Move from concrete to general, not from general to concrete; encourage questioning of general principles; build up relationships. • Remotivate to further learning.

Figure 3.6 The learning episode, from Rogers (1986)

- to focus upon day-to-day effects or short-term perspectives;
- to be isolated from meaningful professional interaction with other adults;
- to exhaust their energy; to limit their opportunities for sustained reflection about what they do; and
- 'to increase their dependence upon the experiential knowledge necessary for day-to-day coping to the exclusion of sources of knowledge beyond their immediate classroom' (Fullan, 1991, p33–4).

Change promotes *disclosure* (of thinking and practice) and *feedback*. Change is not an event, but a process:

(Fullan and Stiegelbauer, 1991, p48)

The curriculum leader must support colleagues at all stages of this process, and recognise in doing so that:

> The personal costs of trying new innovations are often high . . . They require one to believe that they will ultimately bear fruit and be worth the personal investment, often without the hope of an immediate return. Costs are also high. The amount of energy and time required to learn the new skills or roles associated with the new innovation is a useful index to the magnitude of resistance.
>
> (House, 1974, p73, in Fullan and Stiegelbauer, 1991)

Michael Fullan's analysis of change led him to identify ten 'do' and 'don't' assumptions which may provide a basis for your thinking about leading change through staff development.

Assumptions about change

1. Do not assume that your version of what the change should be is the one which should or could be implemented. One of the main purposes of the process of implementation is to 'exchange your reality'.
2. Significant change involves a certain amount of ambiguity, ambivalence, and uncertainty for the individual. So effective implementation is a process of clarification. It requires colleagues to work out their own meanings in practice.

3. Conflict and disagreement are inevitable and fundamental to successful change. Smooth implementation may be a sign that not much is really changing.

4. People need pressure to change, but this will only really be effective under conditions which encourage reaction and inter-action, and where support is available as well as challenge.

5. Effective change takes time. Persistence is a critical attribute of successful change.

6. Lack of implementation is not necessarily outright rejection or resistance to change.

7. Do not expect all or even most people or groups to change. Instead of being discouraged by all that remains to be done, be encouraged by what has been accomplished by way of improvement resulting from your actions.

8. Assume that you will need a plan which takes account of these assumptions, based on a knowledge of the change process.

9. Assume that no amount of knowledge will ever make it totally clear what action should be taken.

10. Assume that particular innovations will and should affect the culture of the whole institution.

(Fullan, 1991, p105–107)

Thinking about managing relationships with colleagues

People trust people who are predictable, whose positions are known and who keep at it; leaders who are trusted make themselves known, make their positions clear.

(Bennis and Nanus, 1985)

In their study of leadership, Bennis and Nanus identified five key skills:

- the ability to accept people as they are;
- the capacity to approach relationships and problems in terms of the present rather than the past;
- the ability to treat those who are close to them with the same courteous attention that they would extend to strangers and casual acquaintances. (Two problems of over familiarity cited are (1) not hearing what is said, and (2) failing to provide feedback which indicates attentiveness);
- the ability to trust others even if the risk is great;

● the ability to do without constant approval and recognition from others.

(Bennis and Nanus, 1985, p66–7)

ACTIVITY 3.4

1. Estimate your own abilities in each of these skill areas by assessing yourself on a 1–5 scale of effectiveness, and providing *one example* of your behaviour with a colleague or colleagues in situations which demonstrate the *application* of each of these skills.
2. When you have done this, discuss the results with a trusted colleague.

Michael Fullan suggests ten guidelines for action:

1. Avoid 'if only' statements, externalising the blame and other forms of wishful thinking;
2. Start small, think big. Don't overmanage;
3. Focus on something concrete and important eg curriculum or teaching;
4. Focus on something fundamental eg of professional significance to school development or of personal significance;
5. Practise fearlessness and other forms of risk-taking;
6. Empower others;
7. Build a vision relevant to both goals and change processes;
8. Decide what you are not going to do;
9. Build allies;
10. Know when to be courteous.

(Fullan, 1992, p35)

Managing relationships with colleagues

You will have noticed that it is communication, planning and interpersonal skills which are constantly highlighted in the literature on effective leadership. 'Person' management is clearly a special skill. We have all met the 'stone age obstructionist' colleague who does not see the need for change and has no desire to do so. Managing change is difficult, as Machiavelli recognised many years ago.

> There is nothing more difficult to carry out, nor more doubtful of success, nor more dangerous to handle than to initiate a new order of things. For the reformer has enemies in all who profit by the old order, and only lukewarm defenders in all those who would profit by the new order. The lukewarmness arises partly from fear of their adversaries who have law in their favour, and partly from the incredulity of mankind who do not truly believe in anything new until they have had actual experience of it.
>
> (Machiavelli, 1513)

So we must recognise that change will involve tensions if not conflict. More importantly, we must also recognise that, however committed, knowledgeable or skilled you are, however high the quality of learning opportunities presented to colleagues, however participatory the style of leadership, not everyone will change. The reasons for this will vary. They may range from the values centred genuine professional disagreement, to the spurious lack of respect for a curriculum leader who has less overall teaching experience. Unwillingness or inability to change may have its source in the out-of-school life of the teacher (which may be stressed), in a lack of confidence in developing new teaching approaches, or in a personality clash.

> There was frequently a sense of unease by the class teachers as to why they had been singled out for 'support'. Was it because their teaching was regarded as inadequate, or because they were a 'soft target' on the staff.
>
> (Sullivan, 1991, p47)

Although this was an external change agent, an advisory teacher, writing about his experience, there is a cautionary note for internal leaders of change too. An invitation to 'be developed' may be seen to imply a weakness or inadequacy. It should be recognised that teaching is a personal as well as a professional business, so that:

- it is not always easy to receive help;
- it is difficult to commit oneself to change;
- it is difficult to submit oneself to the influence of a helper: help is a threat to self esteem, integrity and independence;
- it is not easy to see one's problems clearly at first;
- sometimes problems seem too large, too overwhelming, or too unique to share easily;
- it is not easy to trust a stranger and be open with him or her.

> (Egan, 1982)

So trust and the *timing* of interventions for staff development are important, and relationships crucial where development activities are school-based and school-led. It is important, then, for the curriculum leader to take account of the various *personal* as well as institutional contexts in which (s)he offers support. As Fullan has pointed out:

> Educational change depends on what teachers do and think – it's as simple and complex as that.
>
> (Fullan, 1983, p55)

The curriculum leader, therefore, needs to strive for 'win–win' situations and avoid battles over personal status. This is not to say that conflict should be avoided. On the contrary, it is the sine qua non of change, and can be used as a creative force.

The non-rational world of change

There is little point, then, in pretending that curriculum change is an entirely rational process. Implicit in the process of identifying, defining and solving curriculum problems are processes of *personal change*, what Patrick Easen (1985) called 'perspective transformation', seeing the world in new ways which necessitates:

- reflecting upon our present practice;
- challenging familiar assumptions which influence that practice;
- exploring new ways of acting in accord with how we now view reality.

(Easen, 1985, p130)

Allied to curriculum and personal change is interpersonal change, which is 'concerned with the *process* of effective communication, so that mutual support may be sought and given through self-disclosure and feedback' (Easen, 1985, p130).

Whilst much of the curriculum leader's work will be in one-to-one situations, a good deal of it will occur through small group meetings, and we have written about this in Chapter Two.

There are many kinds of difficult responses which you will have to manage during your role as curriculum leader in meetings (including your own!). Here are some:

> *The dominant person:* 'As I was saying, the *only* solution is *mine.*'
> *The long-winded person:* 'Well, you could look at it this way etc (5 minutes), but there again,' (5 minutes).

The quiet, inhibited person: 'It's a good idea, but I don't think I'm any good at this.'

The angry, bitter person: 'It means more work, and for what? There's no promotion in it for me.'

The action replay: 'Before going ahead, I think we should look again at the basis for the decision taken at the last meeting.'

The democrat: 'We need more time and data – and we should consult more people before taking the final decision.'

(Based on Bulman, 1986, p31)

It is possible to plan at least to minimise the potentially destructive force of many of these kinds of responses at meetings by keeping a checklist which will enable you to:

- envision what is going to happen;
- limit the participants;
- define your own role in the discussion;
- limit issues;
- prepare a working agenda;
- arrive early;
- break down any barriers between yourself and the group;
- start on time;
- make a good beginning;
- get announcements out of the way early and quickly;
- state the purpose, objectives and estimated duration time;
- restate the objective of the meeting periodically;
- represent the group to the group by reflective behaviour;
- appear impartial;
- separate fact from opinion to the meeting;
- watch the pacing;
- be on the lookout for emotional build ups;
- seek contributions;
- make people feel important;
- clarify;
- take things step by step;
- protect the weak;
- divide problems;
- keep the meeting moving;
- end the meeting clearly and neatly.

(Keiffer, 1988)

During the meetings themselves you will need to be aware of colleagues who may adopt personal roles which will hinder progress. Timm and Peterson (1982) have identified some of these:

Personal roles:
1. *Blocking.* Constantly raises objections, insists nothing can be done, introduces irrelevant digression.
2. *Aggression.* Deflates status of others, expresses disapproval and ill-will.
3. *Recognition-seeking.* Boasts, calls attention to self, seeks sympathy or pity, claims credit for ideas.
4. *Confessing.* Engages in personal catharsis and uses group as audience for mistakes.
5. *Clowning.* Diverts attention of group to tangents, engages in horseplay and ridicule, disrupts with cynical comment.
6. *Dominating.* Gives directions, orders people, interrupts and insists on own way.
7. *Special interest pleading.* Supports personal projects and interests, presses others for support, acts as representative or advocate for other groups.

(p273)

You will need, therefore, to support the purposes of the meeting by:

- calling for agreement;
- giving reasons why there should be agreement;
- comparing and contrasting options;
- judging or evaluating ideas and options;
- clarifying and testing views expressed;
- assessing the strength of feelings;
- establishing and reiterating goals.   (Mulholland, 1991, p186)

Who is to blame?

Feelings of powerlessness which contribute to teachers' lowered sense of efficacy are often brought about in systems where they have little control over what is taught. Of course, the most creative and dynamic teachers will always find ways of resisting curriculum guidelines and adopting them to suit their own purposes. But the reality for most ordinary teachers is that they do not. For them, detailed guidelines are not frameworks of opportunity but prisons of constraint.

(Fullan and Hargreaves, 1992, p48)

Finally, it is necessary to recognise that the change occurs within a broad educational and political context. The career development structures for teachers ensure, for example, that the vast majority will not achieve promotion from the class teacher grade; and the economic situation of the time may make change of school difficult. Fullan and Hargreaves (1992) identify six basic problems for those engaged in involving colleagues in development activities:

1. Overload (the sheer increase in volume and complexity of tasks).
2. Isolation (from colleagues).
3. Group think (where individual ideas/opinions/ideals are compromised for the sake of consensus).
4. Untapped competence (as a result of isolation in practice and few previous developmental opportunities).
5. Narrowness in the teacher's role (experience of one age group, no experience of leadership roles).
6. Poor solutions and failed reform (cynicism as a result of previous ill-thought-out, unsuccessful change attempts).

(Adapted from Fullan and Hargreaves, 1992, p7)

It is as well to remember that classroom teachers may have been denied opportunities to develop over a long period, and that the fifty- (or thirty-) year-old 'timer-server' may have lacked induction support, or school leadership which has taken account in its staff development plan of the need to address, for example, the effect of the ageing process upon energy and motivation, the desire for leadership, or the dissemination of classroom competencies. Saying no, may not always be a sign of pig-headedness.

4

ASSERTIVENESS SKILLS

In this chapter we develop the notion that a core skill for curriculum leaders in schools, be they Headteachers, Deputies or team leaders, is assertiveness. Assertiveness is identified as a term used to define a cluster of social skills necessary for individuals to function productively and interdependently in teams. Assertiveness theory is outlined and readers are encouraged to identify their own habitual patterns of behaviour, passive, aggressive, manipulative or assertive. Exercises specifically designed to encourage self-reflection are provided alongside suggestions for improving interpersonal relationships in work teams.

A fundamental task for primary educators is to facilitate the development of personal autonomy and confidence as life-long learners in their young pupils. Nothing is more important and nothing more complex or rewarding a process. It is quite simply the difference between failing the next generation or providing them with the emotional, social and intellectual tools to build productive, worthwhile lives which have meaning and purpose. Lives for which the truest of measures is what you are and what you can contribute not who you are or how much you can make. The question that we as teachers would wish to pose pupils at both the symbolic and literal levels is: what sort of person do you wish to become and what sort of world do you wish to inherit?

The vehicle for the development of this dialogue is the school curriculum and the engine the relationships which are forged between teachers and their pupils both inside and outside the classroom. Increasingly, those teachers with special responsibility for managing the development of the curriculum in schools have come to acknowledge the responsibility they face in humanising a National Curriculum designed at a central rather than a local or institutional level. This is a particularly knotty challenge for curriculum leaders and the challenge exists at the personal and professional level. For teaching is, at its heart, concerned with the communication of value and the curriculum is a dynamic medium for the transmission of the prevailing superordinate societal and cultural values. It must be the task of teachers to enable pupils to discover a critical pathway through such a curriculum so that they have at least the chance of emerging at the end of their school careers individuals able to make choices and take decisions based upon an evaluation of their rights and responsibilities in a society riddled with injustice and pain.

While the curriculum leader will find much of value written on aspects of the primary curriculum: planning, resourcing, training, assessment, evaluation (Kelly, 1986; Blenkin and Kelly, 1987), less attention is focused on the human relations element of *how* growthful, productive relationships might be engendered in the classroom between teacher and pupil. Still *less* attention is devoted to the means whereby teachers might foster such dynamic, creative working relationships in the staff teams which are responsible for curriculum or staff development.

> conditions that are powerful enough to sustain 'collegial' relationships among teachers require a degree of organisation, energy, skill, and endurance often underestimated in summary reports. A closer look reveals the challenge of organisation and leadership, and uncovers the strains that accompany (and perhaps yield) the triumphs.
>
> (Little, 1984, p84)

The focus of this chapter is on the personal and interpersonal dimension of working in curriculum planning teams and even more directly on the assertiveness or personal effectiveness skills necessary to function fully and creatively in teams convened to take forward school policy, planning and action on curriculum matters. In effect, to borrow Little's (1984) phrase, to 'yield the triumphs' that are the hallmark of successful curriculum planning. We will argue that effective leadership of such teams requires growth oriented, critically reflective individuals who are committed to a way of being in relationships which promotes interdependent working cultures. This seems a particularly pertinent and pressing item for the staff development agenda for members of the teaching profession. In recent years there has been an unprecedented rise in the level of expressed teacher job dissatisfaction. Teachers have regularly and systematically reported to researchers and their professional organisations feeling constantly stressed, even burnt out, out of control of their professional lives, confused, low in morale and under-valued culturally, socially and politically.

There has been evidence of a self-conscious process of systematic disempowerment of the teaching profession. Denied access to the centres of educational policy-making, teachers now have to face with courage the challenge of rediscovering a voice that is centred in principled action and grounded in the belief of educational equality of opportunity for all our children – in spite of the shifting sands of political and educational expediency. The source of such a voice is not easily found. It requires that in Jersild's (1955) phrase 'teachers face themselves' on a journey of creative self-discovery. We would want to add that teachers must first listen to their inner voice before it can be articulated and draw strength from the potency of their own experience. Then it is possible to discover within themselves that what they have to offer young children is not so lightly discarded. Teachers need to learn to believe in themselves again, not uncritically, but as assertive, responsible individuals in pursuit of excellence in schools. The alternative to this reconceptualisation of self is too grim a prospect to contemplate as many teachers are finding to their personal cost.

But how is such a reconceptualisation to be undertaken? How might the teacher as learner equip him or herself for the task? What are the hazards and obstacles that lie on the path? We will investigate the last question first. Anyone who has worked for any length of time in a school will know that it is the *multiplicity of demands* which soak up energy, enthusiasm and commitment even in the most dedicated of teachers. The possible restorative effect of a summer vacation is lost if it proves emotionally difficult to leave behind anxieties about SATs scores, or the horror of National Curriculum documentation at the classroom door. However, we would argue that, despite the task of putting in place the bureaucratic machinery of the National Curriculum, the single most *emotionally and physically* draining task is the essential participation in hundreds and hundreds of complex verbal and non-verbal communications in any one working day. From the school nurse to the social worker, the police man/woman to the parent, the LEA official to the school inspector, the local secondary school to the community action group and all this before teachers even set foot inside the classroom door. Many teachers will report with absolute conviction (if somewhat defensively) that they have an almost magical ability to listen to or participate in several conversations at once.

> Start reading, Jane. Yes, you can go to the toilet, Mark. I thought I told you two to put the gerbils back in their cage. No, it is not time to play in the Lego, Julie. Ow! That was my toe Charlie. Sam please tell Mr Harris we are ready for PE now. Lovely reading Jane.

or,

> Just a minute Jenny, I need to have a chat with you about school camp. Hold on though there's Arthur, I must ask him if he's got the computer in his classroom. Will you give Tom's mother a reminder that she said she would help out at the craft fair and by the way, you are coming to the Bring and Buy on Saturday aren't you? Good. Oh, Arthur!

While most of us would recognise similar patterns of interaction, the emotional juggling act necessary to keep so many relationships spinning in the air is enormous. One bad day, or more realistically week or term, can send the whole shaky edifice crashing down. What is clear is that relationships need nurturing in order to develop. Teachers need to learn how to nurture themselves if they are to develop. What are the key constituents of healthy, growthful relationships? Carl Rogers (1962) provided us with a most elegant and concise answer to this question, the result of a lifetime engagement with the puzzle. As with many puzzles the solution that he found was delightfully simple. He tentatively proposed that

- empathy
- positive regard
- genuineness or authenticity

were the *core conditions* necessary if relationships were to be facilitative or in his terms therapeutic. The core conditions are not absolutes nor did he claim that they were definitive, instead they are meant to be understood as a set of processes that we might struggle with moment by moment if we truly desire to be partners in healthier relationships than we are right here and now. What is the leap from Rogers' work to assertiveness training? Increased assertiveness or personal effectiveness in relationships is one of the means that individuals can employ to become in Rogers' terms (1978) fully functioning people. Assertiveness training provides a simple set of behavioural tools to enable us to move closer to that ideal self in relationships. A person who can really listen with respect to other people's points of view, express feelings in a way which moves relationships forward not backwards, say what she wants but be clear that it is not the final word and have the courage to give feedback honestly and to take it with gratitude. These are some of the means by which we can measure our present level of effectiveness in relationships.

'Life is difficult', as Scott Peck (1978) so pithily reminds us and it would be naive to underplay the degree of difficulty in becoming more assertive in our daily lives. For many of us feel from time to time that getting what we want out of life can be a problem. For others knowing what we want from life can be equally difficult. We might experience being trapped in relationships which we know to be unhealthy but do not have the necessary courage to extricate ourselves. We might be dimly aware that there are feelings which we must not or dare not express if people are to continue to like us. Conversely, some people experience being so full of feeling that it is almost impossible for them to contain it and so express the feelings in bursts of temper, rages or sulks.

From time to time articulating clearly and assertively what we want or what we feel appears difficult for all of us. In our social or familial lives while unassertive behaviours such as these will undoubtedly prove problematic, it is in our professional role that they appear in sharper, more urgent focus. The role of middle manager or curriculum leader in a primary school requires us to be skilful communicators in order to perform the role effectively. So it is necessary to examine the following questions. Where do these blocks to self-awareness and self-expression originate? How can we learn to be different? How can we learn to be more fully in touch with feelings and thoughts and express them in positive, relationship building ways? What range of skills would be required for a primary teacher with responsibilities for curriculum leadership? We will explore these questions and offer some self-help strategies for learning to behave in more assertive ways.

What is assertiveness?

We will argue that assertiveness is not merely a communication style but a *way of life*. Assertiveness is the lifelong *dedication* to pursuing the goal of open, truthful, clear communication in interpersonal relationships. The *ability* to be in touch with and express feelings and thoughts as they are experienced and the *courage* to acknowledge that other people in our relationships have the right to be themselves with all the human frailty that implies. These qualities depend upon a high level of *skilled behaviours*, which need to be continually re-examined in the light of experience for their effectiveness and authenticity. This requires awareness, a degree of risk-taking, discipline and a positive self-esteem in short *emotional and intellectual maturity*.

Assertiveness training has its origins in psychotherapy and clinical psychology (Rakos, 1991). Patients undergoing therapy who were identified by clinicians as having insufficient interactional skills to cope with the demands of day-to-day relationships, were rehearsed in the practice of simple communication skills in order to damp down overly aggressive responses or to help build up the confidence to initiate social interaction. Such individuals often were consumed with anxiety or depression to the extent that they were debilitated from behaving in their own best interests and the interests of others. Already many readers will recognise that such a cluster of feelings and behaviours is not merely confined to those individuals undergoing clinical treatment and that such therapeutic approaches would be useful in the classroom with students (Kutnick, 1991) as well as for teachers in the staffroom (Gordon, 1974). In fact, Rakos (in Hargie, 1986) cites multiple examples of training manuals for assertiveness skills aimed at women, children, job employers and employees as well as the public at large.

This plethora of assertiveness training now on offer is aimed at individuals from the 'well' population and the training is almost always undertaken in a group context. The transition from locating such therapeutic interventions firmly in the clinical, treatment-centred domain to the self-help, self-empowerment, personal growth milieu was largely a result of the women's movement in the 1960s and 1970s (Dickson, 1982). Despite borrowing heavily from therapeutic assertiveness training approaches, women's groups tended to focus primarily on the issues of personal rights, values, the effects of patriarchy on personal effectiveness and raising the self-esteem of women. Personal effectiveness, a term used synonymously with assertiveness training came to be used by many women who experienced the misappropriation of the term 'assertive woman' into a term of personal abuse and social derision. Reclaiming and retitling the work personal effectiveness in itself was viewed as an assertive act by many women who reported feeling systematically disempowered from childhood and wished to challenge the traditional

ACTIVITY 4.1

Are you ready to be assertive?
Read the following statements and decide how many are true for you in
your life right now and then try the exercise printed below.

- I am always open and honest with the people in my life.
- I stand up for my rights and the rights of others.
- I am able to express my thoughts and feelings with confidence to
  those in authority and to those I have authority over.
- I can refuse unreasonable requests assertively.
- I am able to both give and receive feedback in constructive ways.
- I manage my time so that my own personal and professional de-
  velopment needs are given attention.
- I am aware that I have shortcomings but that I can change.
- I have clear goals and priorities in my life but I am willing to negoti-
  ate them if circumstances change.
- My body posture is relaxed and healthy. My body expresses what I
  am saying congruently.
- Failure now means learning how to succeed in the future.
- I am able to apologise.
- I am able to forgive.
- I am self-disciplined.
- I take responsibility for my own actions.
- Each time I face my fear I grow as a person.

Self-reflection activity
1. Make a note of any of the statements which you felt particularly
   difficult for you to own. You may wish to spend some time reflecting on the emotional aspects linked to the difficulty. What prevents
   you from behaving in this way?
2. What do you imagine the outcomes will be if you do behave more
   assertively?
3. Positively celebrate the statements which you can wholeheartedly
   claim for yourself.
4. Choose two or three statements which you would like to work on
   claiming as true for you and start now.

cultural stereotypes afforded to women through the engagement with
assertiveness training (Ernst and Goodison, 1981). However it is entirely
possible to work through a schedule of self-help assertiveness training
through a structured learning programme. The remainder of this chapter
will focus on such self-help strategies for primary teachers with management responsibility in relation to curriculum development. We would

encourage the reader to actively engage with the exercises provided in order to clarify firstly, your own dominant or preferred modes of interpersonal behaving, secondly, what behaviour changes are desirable and necessary and, thirdly, planning for change.

We learn about social behaviour at first from our personal experiences in a family group. We learn quickly in this group and sometimes painfully that behaviours, feelings, responses fall into two broad categories – acceptable and unacceptable. The former bring approval, affirmation, love and confirmation of our sense of ourselves as worthwhile human beings; the latter disapproval, negation, punishment and the creation of uncertainty and anxiety at the core of our being. However such is the capriciousness of human behaviour that rewards and punishments are never as clearly delineated as the above descriptor would lead us to believe. Nevertheless, it becomes clear that over time a pattern of conditioned emotional responding is established (Hall and Hall, 1988) which takes awareness and effort in equal measures for the individual to break down in adult life. Assertiveness theorists tell us (Lange and Jakubowski, 1976) that dysfunctional behaviour responses fall into three discrete but overlapping categories: the *passive* response, the *manipulative* (or indirect aggressive) response and the *aggressive* response. The healthy functional behaviour category is described as *assertive* and the aim of any assertiveness skills training is first of all to determine which of these categories best exemplifies the individual's preferred, learned mode of responding. At this stage it is worth bearing in mind that these behaviours are theorised as existing along a continuum of the individual's behavioural repertoire and that all of us will in different social contexts respond in very different ways (Rakos, 1991). For example, a teacher may respond aggressively to a male Headteacher but passively with the female school secretary. Virginia Satir (1972) makes the point that it is when we feel stressed or under pressure that we are least likely to behave assertively and will generally regress to a tried and tested defensive style of behaving, passively, aggressively or manipulatively.

> To gain in knowledge of self, one must have the courage to seek it and the humility to accept what one may find.
>
> (Jersild, 1955)

ACTIVITY 4.2

Self-assessment schedule
Thoroughly familiarise yourself with the following set of descriptors and try to reflect honestly upon which types of behaviour best describe your own. You may wish to confer with a trusted friend or partner about your own perceptions or judgements. If you do this remember that they have a right to a point of view and an assertive response would be to thank them for giving the feedback, while retaining the right to have your own feelings and opinions about its validity.

Then try the exercise outlined in Activity 4.3.

The passive type

Internalised messages from childhood

- Keep quiet
- Keep smiling
- Don't complain
- Anger is a punishable offence – feelings are dangerous
- What the authorities say goes
- My views aren't important
- No one listens to me
- Be a peacemaker

Adult communication style characterised by

- Low verbal input in groups
- Inappropriate smiling, excessive politeness or obsequiousness
- Absence of feeling statements in communication
- Fear of initiating interactions
- Anxiety about the worth of personal contribution
- Unable to feel or express anger
- Doesn't know or can't say what she wants
- Voice sounds distant, unconnected to feelings

Body posture communicates

- Lack of self-confidence

- Shrinking away
- Supplicating
- Limp, vapid, lacking in good muscle tone
- Difficulty in making and maintaining eye contact
- Allows others to intrude on personal space

Patterns of negative reactions from others

- Ignores or even forgets their presence
- Views easily dismissed
- Undervalued
- Walked all over
- Easily manipulated
- Passivity interpreted as weakness
- Shown little respect

Leadership style

- Unable to make decisions independently
- Mistakes consensus for management
- Finds communicating a sense of vision tough
- Easily influenced by the strong expression of feeling
- Tries to damp down conflict between group members
- Pretends feelings will go away

Needs to work on

- Building self-esteem. Learning to love herself
- Believing in personal rights
- Getting in touch with the courage to face responsibility
- Listening to feelings, her own and other people's without hiding
- Learning to refuse unreasonable requests – saying no and meaning it
- Staying firm under pressure, maintaining personal boundaries
- Upright body posture, calm but firm tone of voice
- Smiling only when appropriate

The manipulative or indirectly aggressive type

Internalised messages from childhood

- I am worthless
- So is everyone else
- Trust no one
- I must be guilty (of something)
- Feelings must be hidden
- They are out to get me: get them first

Adult communication style characterised by

- Circumlocution, rarely identifying what it is they really want
- Avoidance of the personal pronoun 'I'. Uses 'one', 'they' 'most people'
- Uses guilt as a means of getting others to do what they want
- Hides real feelings and motives
- Difficult to pin down
- May use a mixture of threats, praise, sarcasm, promises to get their own way
- Slippery

Body posture communicates

- Fixed facial expression, usually smile or grin
- Eyes give little away
- Shiftiness
- Wheedling
- Personal boundaries shifting
- Failure must be hidden

Patterns of negative reactions from others

- Wariness
- Suspicion
- Feeling trapped
- Resentment
- Feeling foolish, stupid or simple-minded

- Frustration about never penetrating the surface layer
- Anger at not being trusted
- Confusion, never knowing where you stand

Leadership style

- Politicking
- Game-playing, setting people up
- Power games
- Pseudo open or democratic style of management
- Withholds information
- Dislikes owning feelings or opinions in groups
- Alternates rewards and punishments

Needs to work on

- Building a feeling of self-worth
- Dealing with messages of guilt from the past
- Owning statements and using 'I'
- Expressing clear statements of personal preference
- Liking self and others

The aggressive type

Internalised messages from childhood

- Stand up for yourself
- Grow up
- It's a tough world out there
- If you want something fight for it
- Big boys/girls don't cry
- Expressing negatives – good, expressing positives – risky
- Avoid exposure or expressing vulnerability

Adult communication style characterised by

- Blaming others
- Raised voice
- Harsh or shrill tone of voice

- Angry, piercing or fixed eye contact
- Constant criticism, dogmatism, failure to negotiate
- Tight-lipped
- Constant interruption of others

Body posture communicates

- Leaning threateningly forward
- Red-faced
- Bodily tension and hyper-arousal
- Clenched fists
- Tight musculature
- Breath holding and superficial breathing
- Pointed finger
- Invades other people's boundaries

Patterns of negative reactions from others

- Fearfulness
- Avoidance
- Treat aggressive type with kid gloves
- Feel unwanted and not needed
- Feel diminished and not valued
- Feel threatened by the possibility of physical violence
- Feel invaded

Leadership style

- Authoritarian – see it my way or else
- Failure not permitted
- Inability to trust the group
- Reluctance to delegate
- Unable to encourage maximum participation because of fear of members

Needs to work on

- Building up empathy
- Letting the other person express a point of view without fear of punishment

- Learning to trust and value people
- Expressing vulnerability
- Owning imperfection and saying sorry
- Lowering the volume of the voice
- Expressing feelings as they are experienced without letting them build up to bursting point

The assertive type

Internalised messages from childhood

- I have something to offer
- I can do it
- I am a lovable person
- I have rights, so do other people
- It's OK to express my feelings
- I can trust people
- Failing is not the end of the world
- I take responsibility for my own actions

Adult communication style characterised by

- Ability to listen, even to hostile viewpoints
- Will stick with it when the going gets tough
- Can express unpopular opinions
- Sense of humour
- Able to refuse unreasonable requests
- Can request behaviour change in others
- Expresses feeling and encourages others to do so too
- Gives and receives compliments

Body posture communicates

- Fluidity, relaxed hand and arm gestures
- Ability to initiate and maintain comfortable eye contact
- Open, frank expression
- Warmth
- Genuineness, a match between the verbal and nonverbal messages
- Confident, firm tone of voice

ACTIVITY 4.3

Take a moment or two to relax as you prepare to spend some time learning more about yourself. Now cast your mind back over the last few months at school and recall any incidents where you experienced a conflict of interest with a colleague or colleagues which resulted in an unsatisfactory verbal exchange for you. The memories might come back quickly, or they may take a little time. Now jot down the memories from *three* significant incidents which left you feeling uneasy, hurt, misunderstood or guilty. Try to recall the feelings that were around for you before, during and after the incidents took place. If you can, even remember the actual words spoken. Use your visual memory to picture the scenes and visualise your own body posture and that of the other participants during the episodes.

Now return to the descriptors of types and see if your behaviours and those of your colleagues match any of the categories. If your own behaviour fell outside of the assertiveness category try to replay the scene in imagination, this time paying attention to the following;

- What do I want from this interaction?
- What do I really want to say?
- How might I encourage the other person to say what he/she wants?
- I am in touch with my feelings but they are under control.
- I can maintain comfortable eye contact.
- My body is alert yet relaxed.
- I am prepared to express my point of view and listen to my colleague without interruption.
- If I feel strongly, I can express the feelings without experiencing loss of face.
- I am prepared to offer feedback to my colleague about his/her behaviour if I believe this would improve our understanding of the situation. I am prepared to receive feedback in the same way.

Remember to visualise each scene in turn. The events leading up to it, during and immediately afterwards. Pay close attention to your *feelings, posture, words and tone of voice*. This is how it feels to be assertive. Keep that image and those feelings. They will come back to you when you need to assert yourself in the future.

Patterns of reactions from others

- Respected for integrity and honesty
- Seen as a role model by others
- Can incur hostility from non-assertive individuals

- May be seen as aggressive rather than assertive if a woman
- Might be placed in the role of saviour by dependent colleagues

Leadership style

- Encourages participation and co-operation
- Sees interpersonal conflict in a group as handleable and potentially creative
- Delegates and devolves responsibility
- Clear about personal and role boundaries with self and others
- Believes in principled action
- Actively promotes equal opportunities
- Sees staff development as the cornerstone of success

Needs to work on

- Paying attention to the emotional, physical and spiritual renewal necessary to maintain an assertive life style

Assertive people feel good about themselves. Generally speaking, they were lucky enough to receive positive esteem messages from people who loved them when they were growing up and received positive reinforcement for assertive behaviour. We know that self-concept – the way that we feel about ourselves – affects communication and the way that we behave with others (Burns, 1982, Adler and Towne, 1978). In order to maximise interpersonal effectiveness it is essential for teachers to engage actively in monitoring their self-esteem needs and to set about raising their own evaluation of themselves through committed endeavour. Proactivity is the key. It is not enough as adults to rely on the love and care of others to make us feel good about ourselves; although this is beneficial it is insufficient. We need to experience success which has been achieved through a dynamic or vigorous struggle with difficult learning.

Throughout this chapter we have referred to work or task groups in the primary school as curriculum teams. Teams are not the same as groups. Teams can be defined as a group of individuals brought together by consent to engage with a problem-solving task co-operatively and with a clear vision of what a successful goal or outcome for the team in an institutional context might be. A team would require a high degree of

---

ACTIVITY 4.4

Improve your self-esteem
Discover what you need to grow and start work on it today. These are some strategies which you might find useful.

- Learn to praise yourself
- Don't put yourself down
- Learn to accept compliments
- Learn new skills
- Take care of your body
- Learn yoga or meditation techniques
- Do things for other people
- Break a useless habit
- Engage in personal growth activities
- Talk to trusted friends about difficulties you face

---

autonomy and appropriate resourcing to achieve the desired outcome. Members of the team may have different but complementary skills which need to be harnessed if the team is to achieve its goal. Teams are purposeful and success oriented within their own terms of reference. Teams by implication are not a collection of individuals brought together randomly or haphazardly with covert personal agendas which are superordinate to or at odds with the aims of the team. Emphatically, members of teams need to be or must learn to become socially skilled, assertive individuals. This cannot be left to chance or fortune and it will be necessary for curriculum leaders to foster the conditions in their teams which create generative working relationships. Understanding group processes can go some way to giving a framework for the positive interventions that can be made to help the work of the group remain on course. Tuckman's (1965) four-stage model of group development is useful as an exemplar of how at various stages of the group's life, assertive interventions by the team leader might prove rewarding in the maintenance of team effectiveness.

- forming
- storming
- norming
- performing

Tuckman argues that all groups will inevitably follow this pattern

---

ACTIVITY 4.5

Helping to create an assertive team

The forming stage
Leading a development team, even a small team of three or four colleagues, assertively requires that a culture of openness, safety and trust
is built up from the very first team meeting. This may involve for the
passive leader being much clearer about what he or she wants from the
group. For the aggressive leader it will require less participation, less
dominant interventions, more tentative suggestions and from the manipulative leader a willingness to trust the competence of the group and him
or herself. Generally, there will be a set of pre-existing relationships
which at first you may feel ambivalent about disturbing but it is vital at the
outset to *engage the team in a discussion of ground rules or principles to
guide team behaviour.* From experience such a list often includes items
such as:

- listening
- including all members in the discussion
- keeping a sense of humour
- being honest with each other
- keeping to time
- keeping confidentiality if necessary
- work out all disagreements during the meeting
- don't bottle up feelings or resentments
- pat ourselves on the back from time to time
- it's OK to screw up (some of the time!)

A team exercise such as this will help to lower anxiety levels by encouraging the sharing of feelings and establishing co-operation as a common goal.

---

although the rate at which the group progresses (or regresses) towards
task performance would be impossible to predict. Each stage is characterised by clusters of feelings and patterns of behaviour. The forming
stage is marked by increased levels of member anxiety, tentativeness,
looking for a leader and associated dependent behaviours. When members feel surer of the ground, more familiar with the territory, power
struggles may ensue with the testing out of the designated leader and
pairing of members to create alternative leadership. Blaming or accusing
and inability to accept fully the responsibility of membership are common features. Norming is established when patterns of behaviour, either
helpful or unhelpful, are tacitly accepted by members. Part of the

ACTIVITY 4.6

Weathering the storm

The storming stage

There are a number of ways to help team members use the energy created in the storming stage constructively. Modelling self-disclosure is an important leadership skill and is particularly relevant when feelings may be running high but remain unexpressed. The task then is to use leader self-disclosure, immediacy and challenging as a means of raising the hidden agendas into the consciousness of the group. By paying attention to your own feelings and intuitions at this stage and disclosing anxieties, fears or preoccupations about destructive behaviours within the group, members can be released from the knot of tension created during the storming stage. This release is obtained by asking the group to pay attention to the emotional issues which may be blocking it. The feelings should be expressed as they are felt (immediacy) and voiced in an assertive tone of voice. 'Immediacy refers to the capacity of people to be able to respond immediately to what they are experiencing in a relationship and to say what otherwise might be left unsaid' (Langham and Parker, 1988). If you can offer information freely and unselfconsciously it will encourage other members to express what may be difficult or painful feelings too.

I am feeling increasingly anxious about the way people are interrupting each other and at least two of us haven't managed to get a word in. I really want to understand what the real issue is here, otherwise I don't believe we can move on.

A useful formula for self-disclosure in relation to interaction is

I feel . . . when you/we/I . . .

Firstly, label the feeling. Own the feeling by saying 'I'. If you catch yourself using 'we think', 'one ought', 'you must' and other distancing statements then it is a sure sign that you are slipping back into patterns of unassertive responding. Rationalisations to do with politeness, social convention, immodesty, are usually just that – rationalisations for unassertive behaviour. Next refer to a specific piece of behaviour which prompts the feeling. In this way the other person is clear that this is *your personal perception* and is referring to a *specific piece of behaviour* rather than damning the whole person. There is a good chance that what you say will be experienced as an encouragement to respond rather than a final judgement.

Try this exercise. Think of five people in your life right now where you believe that disclosing your feelings would move the relationship forward. Rehearse the 'I feel . . . when you . . .' formula and then try it out for real. Ensure that you say the sentence assertively with a calm and relaxed posture. Be prepared for a dialogue to begin and that the other person has a right to his/her feelings too. Remember feelings can be positive as well as negative.

ACTIVITY 4.7

Establishing a co-operative culture
The norming stage
Confrontation skills are necessary if leaders are to challenge the emergence of unhelpful group norms by powerful, self-oriented members in the group. The following are a set of skills taken from assertiveness training which can promote leader effectiveness in teams.
Asking for feedback
A request for feedback about your behaviour or leadership in the team creates a situation where members have the opportunity to offer perceptions, positive or negative, without fear of punishment. It also creates a culture where self-appraisal is routine and an accepted part of group behaviour. This also provides an opportunity to clear up misunderstandings or unfinished business. It is important not to be defensive about what is offered as feedback but to accept it for what it is – a valuable piece of information about the way in which you are perceived by other group members.
Win–win negotiation
Inevitably any task group will be involved in a conflict of ideas or interests. What is less inevitable, unfortunately, is that the team leader or team members have the skills to handle disputes creatively. Establishing a win–win culture requires a frame of mind ruthlessly prepared to fight for a workable compromise where the self-respect and rights of individual members are not eroded or hegemonised by more powerful or dominant members. The meta goal of the team must be uppermost when reaching a position which is acceptable to all parties.
Repetition
Sometimes referred to as the broken record technique, this is a technique to be used sparingly and only in very difficult situations, for example when a team member is exploding with rage and destroying the chances for work.
  I want you to sit down now. I want you to sit down now. I want you to sit down now.
Said in a firm, confident tone you can maintain your position in the face of impossibly destructive behaviour, irrational logic or argumentative distraction.

responsibility of the team leader may be to ensure that the evolving group norms are facilitative of individual expression and the performance of team task. A failure by the team leader to confront assertively unhelpful or hostile behaviours in members can result in task performance being carried out without energy, commitment or enthusiasm – basically just going through the motions. On the other hand, the emotional and intellectual satisfaction which can be derived when a team is committed to person-centred values and ways of working can be intense. When this happens the performance of the task becomes a

---

ACTIVITY 4.8

Celebrating success
The performing stage
Although doing a job well is in itself a psychologically enriching experience, a powerful leader contribution is to reinforce positive contributions with public acknowledgement of an appropriate nature. If like us you have groaned at the long list of staff and parents thanked by the head for the school play you will know that this is not what is meant by appropriate. Leaders need to find both formal and informal ways of celebrating a job well done and there also needs to be a way that staff development is closely linked to the outcome of the task. So that members of the team can be clear about what their strengths are and how they can become stronger by learning new skills or ways of working.

---

rewarding, refreshing experience which in itself is experienced as pleasurable. The satisfaction of a job well done. The challenge for the team leader is to behave in assertive ways which bring the group nearer to this goal.

In this chapter we have argued that teachers need to constantly interrogate their own sense of themselves as contributing members of collegial groups or teams in primary schools. This means a willingness to engage in personal growth and professional renewal. By understanding what it means to lead an assertive life it is possible to reflect critically upon the patterns of learned behaviours and responding which presently may be hindering our interpersonal relationships not enhancing them. We have seen that what is needed is to build self-esteem through strategies such as 'bills of rights', mental rehearsal of assertive responses in difficult situations, relaxation, stress reduction, cognitive restructuring and learning to give and receive feedback. Any teacher who is able to demonstrate such a repertoire of sophisticated social skills would be a good role model indeed for the pupils in their charge and their colleagues in the staffroom. As Albert Schweitzer reminds us, 'Example is leadership'.

PART II

CURRICULUM VALUES AND PRACTICES

5

CURRICULUM PERSPECTIVES: CONTENT AND PROCESS

This chapter is about the balance required between content and process in the curriculum. Starting from a discussion of the nature of schooling, it looks at the dangers inherent in too glib an approach to defined curricula arguing that a proper balance between process and content is especially important when working with young children. It suggests that Britain is now seriously out of step with developments in the rest of the world; and it points to the dangers in too narrow a curriculum driven by inadequate concepts of assessment. Its aim is to provide a stimulus to assist leaders to review their understanding of 'developmentally appropriate practice', and for an appreciation that the medium can be as important as the message.

The curriculum

The school curriculum is a complex concept. It usually purports to be a framework of subjects, ideas, projects or areas of knowledge that can be thought of in progression and placed in a framework of delineated content. Attached to that content are, sometimes, certain processes deemed desirable in ensuring that learning takes place and the curricular goals achieved. In essence that is the assumed position. But, in reality, the curriculum is not always like that; certainly not so for many of the recipients. The 'map of experience', that is, where the curriculum connects and where it is going, is not always clear to the learner. One author vividly recalls the years of Latin at school. For many years he was convinced that all that Latin was about was of countless Roman soldiers falling into ditches and scrambling out by the end of the lesson. By the time the next lesson came there they were back in another ditch again! He began to wonder what the purpose of it all was and why the Romans appeared so stupid. He had no *map* of Caesar's Gallic Wars in his mind, no conceptual apparatus to deal with them and precious little motivation, other than some future examination!

Clearly, the *content* of that far distant lesson had been designed for some purpose; and presumably by someone who had a very clear idea of the progression, continuity, increasing sophistication and conceptual grasp required. But little of it was available to that child, the learner. Add to that a teaching method which frightened him or, in the jargon, a transaction which dominated, and there was relatively little chance of the content reaching the learner in its desired shape.

The term curriculum is itself a metaphor and to it have accrued many others. Some of these metaphors are reminiscent of nutrition. We can read curriculum writers who talk of children being provided with 'a balanced diet'. Some too have warned us against too much 'forced feeding'. Others have used terms reminiscent of torture, believing that the curriculum should 'stretch' children. Yet others have talked in terms of sport, seeing curricular goals as 'hurdles', and so on. Whilst it is foolish to strain the comparisons, it is very clear that the curriculum metaphors employed *do* give a clue to the underlying philosophy and intentions (Lawton, 1984). What, for instance, are we to make of the current tendency to talk of 'delivering the curriculum'; as if somehow one were a sort of Postman Pat who gave out convenient parcels of knowledge at the appropriate stopping points? At very least this displays a massive ignorance of reality. A curriculum is so often mediated by perception that, with the best will in the world, there becomes a marked difference between the intentions of its designer or 'transmitter' and the appreciation of the recipient. The curriculum is a constant vehicle of negotiation; one so mediated by the experiences of the learners, as well as by the skill, or otherwise, of the teacher, that one cannot divorce the process from the content. To return to the nutritional metaphors, as the National Association for the Education of Young Children (NAEYC) says, 'Without attention given to the interests and preferences of the diner, the nourishing meal may go uneaten' (NAEYC/ NAECS, 1991, p23). All of us are aware, after a moment's reflection, that another element also dominates the way learners deal with the curriculum. We probably remember past methods of teaching, including

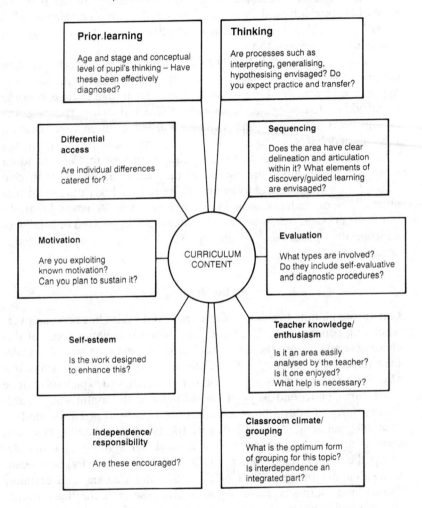

Figure 5.1 'Curriculum content' can be broadly defined, but the learning process may depend more on detailed attention to these ten issues

the personality of the teacher, rather more than the actual *content*. Thus, we might say that the transaction actually overrode the content. Both the prime points are obvious and simple. The state of the learners and what they perceive, need and focus upon, together with the personal style or method adopted by the teacher are likely to be massively influential on the content. To presume that defined content leads to defined outcomes is extremely foolish.

The above comment is simply to represent a debate which has been common for years in the literature of educationists, but is still not fully appreciated by many of the politicians who, from time to time, become involved in actually legislating about curricula and their purposes. Some twenty years ago Eisner and Vallance warned of three very common fallacies in debates on the curriculum. One was to assume that there was a *best* curriculum for all children; another to assume that *how* children learn was more important than *what* they learn; another was to give *content* pre-eminence and to assume there to be a body of content that all children, or students, should master (Eisner and Vallance, 1974). As the NAEYC says, rich, meaningful content should go hand in hand with appropriate processes which utilise developmental knowledge accordingly.

The 'basics'

One of the abiding problems of the last two decades has been an overwhelming concern with 'the basics'. In Western societies some of this clearly stemmed from the disenchantment following the so-called Coleman Report of 1966 in the USA (Coleman et al, 1966). But much of it is also tied to the attempts of post-industrial societies to explain economic down-turns or to find ways of expressing a more contingent, or utilitarian, form of education more fitted for a post-industrial, or modern technological society. At the end of the twentieth century, however, even a modest acquaintance with educational systems in other developed countries makes one aware that Britain (especially) now seems somewhat out of step. Parts of the USA and Canada, and certainly France and Germany, have begun to dispense with the 'back-to-the-basics' ideologies and are recognising once again that there is an important partnership between content and process which is vital to the health of a good education system and may well be vital to its economic and social well-being as well. Indeed, as Britain begins to assemble a curriculum more and more reminiscent of that laid down for Grammar schools in 1904, as we begin to claim that testing lies at the heart of learning, other societies are beginning to re-assert the importance of process and creativity, of change and re-adaptation. The sad fact is that, despite the fulminations and recriminations of the Black Paper writers of the 1960s and 1970s, large parts of British education (and notably the primary sector) *were* in fairly good heart and may now have become more limiting places *after* the 'reforms'. Certainly, there is ample evidence that the British state primary schools were not hotbeds of anarchy or of 'left-wing' child-centred approaches, as many of the Black Paper writers asserted. For the most part British primary schools have been concerned to spend substantial parts of their time on the basics; moreover much of these were taught through typical teacher-directed whole-class methods. But the ideologies of certain groups have clearly prevailed; and the result of fierce campaigning, fuelled, it might be argued, by long and bitter diatribes in some organs of the right-wing press, was the British Education Reform Act of 1988. Since then there has been a preoccupation with prescribed curricula and with testing, such that those calling for a respectful attention to process are in danger of being forgotten.

Such a compression of historical and social forces as that which we have just given is, of course, dangerously simplistic. All education systems are dynamic. They have constantly to seek for a balance between the cultural repository of the indigenous people and those of the pressing needs of the economic and social state of the country, including its immigrant population, its changing international role, and so on. None of this is easy. Too much attention to the culture, history and glories of the past and the educational system becomes static and inward-looking. Too much attention to the dynamics of change and the system becomes rootless and lacking in identity and continuity. A balance is essential.

Purpose and process

In David Orr's commencement address at Arkansas College (1990) there is a clear defence of the purpose of education and, importantly, of the importance of process in it all. He says of adult students, 'Courses taught as lecture courses tend to induce passivity. Indoor classes create the illusion that learning only occurs inside four walls isolated from what students call without apparent irony the "real world". Dissecting frogs in biology classes teaches lessons about nature that no one would verbally profess. Campus architecture is crystallised pedagogy that often reinforces passivity, monologue, domination and artificiality. My point is simply that students are being taught in various and subtle ways beyond the content of courses.' (Orr, op cit) Orr regards subject matter as the tool. The purpose of his address is to reassert the basic principles of education, one of which is that the goal of education is not so much mastery of a particular subject as mastery of one's own person. Another, that responsibility for oneself and for others is so much more important than the 'bottom line' of competition.

Process and developmentally appropriate practice

At its most basic, teaching is about explaining, helping, encouraging children to see meanings and implications in what is under investigation. It may focus on a particular subject content, upon an object; it may set up systems for independent investigation by the child or student, but in the end it must recognise that learning itself is a very varied activity. Furthermore the results may be different from those intended. In short, teachers have to find ways of gradually transferring the responsibility for learning from themselves to the pupils. The Australian Schools Council reports on extensive research findings concerning teaching. They summarise these as follows:

Effective teaching involves

- the establishment of challenging and clear expectations;
- well-organised and structured presentations of content, *relating it to what the children already know* (our italics);
- making optimal use of learning time;
- active and positive interaction between the teacher and students, including questioning to encourage understanding and providing guidance on how to improve work;
- constantly rewarding achievement.

(Schools Council, 1990, p50)

Whilst constantly emphasising the importance of 'rich content', 'appropriate content', and so on, the Council repeatedly refer to the process being one that relies on knowledge of the children and that 'Teachers need to appreciate that process and content of learning are inextricably interwoven, and that an education, or view of education, which concentrates excessively on either one or the other is unsatisfactory' (op cit, p55).

Assessment in perspective

It should be clear from the discussion thus far that we are not anti-content, nor are we anti-assessment. We believe that teachers teach somebody *something*. We do not believe that it is satisfactory to draw up the map of experience after the event, as it were. Teachers need to be sophisticated and skilful in their use of diagnostic assessment so that they can better match and monitor appropriate learning responses. Like those who wrote the TGAT Report (Department of Education and Science, 1988), we share the belief that schools function best when they *plan, do and review*. But we do not think (as apparently did those writing the TGAT Report) that assessment lies at the heart of learning. In that respect we think that the Plowden Report had the emphasis right and had interpreted the (then existing) research correctly. The *child* lies at the heart of learning. This is what Elkind, Bredekamp and others mean when they refer to 'developmentally based practice' or 'developmentally appropriate curricula' (Elkind, 1989). These terms can be best summed up as meaning that above all the curriculum cannot be purely externally determined, imposed in its entirety from outside. Curricula must take into account the entering characteristics of the learners and modify the content (or, if you prefer, *mediate* it through processes which render it more carefully suited to the learner). The problem is that such processes often make a nonsense of 'short, sharp' tests. They make comparison of outcomes and 'outputs' (interesting metaphor from industry) very, very inappropriate. Such assumptions as those of the NAEYC, or of Elkind, or indeed of Bennett on grouping procedures (Bennett, 1990), begin to suggest that the medium has to be varied and may well alter the message (content), at least for the time being. All this is probably very inconvenient for those who would appear to have very simplistic models of input–output approaches to the curriculum, and, one suspects, to the comparison of schools as units of analysis!

Those persons working within early childhood education, that period commonly defined as from birth to 9 years, are dealing with beings whose physical, cognitive and affective growth is of staggering proportions and implications. At probably no other time is the human organism taking in so much; learning, doing, finding out, owning, wondering, joining, and so on. Whilst this may be but the crudest of caricatures, it is clearly what one sees and experiences when among a pre-school group or primary class. To be with children of this age is sometimes to observe expansion of ideas and conceptual leaps which are as impressive as anything seen at post-graduate level. To be with children of this age can be undeniably exciting; it is also totally consuming and often emotionally draining. It can be surprisingly intellectually demanding, with questions of the 'why' sort which would tax a first-class philosopher. But, above all, to be among such a group for any length of time makes one very aware of the danger in seeing curriculum content and its assessment as somehow totally able to be fashioned outside of the children. It is not that primary teachers are especially perverse, or that they all like to be thought of as modestly child-centred ('Dewey-eyed', as some North American commentators call it); rather, it is the undeniable pressure of observation 'in the field' which forces one to acknowledge the vastly different perceptions which greet, process, internalise and make anew any ideas which are provided by the teacher. This implies that teachers cannot wholly structure, create or 'deliver' the precise chains of knowledge. It means that the processes of learning intervene in different places and at different times for different children. It means that teachers have to link, to follow apparent red herrings, to abandon certain threads of exposition and to search for others. Moreover, because of the wide developmental range usually found in such classrooms (we have known four year olds just starting to speak coherently, whilst others are already reading quite well), the notion of some uniform presentation of content and of its uniform assimilation is far from reality. No doubt these are some of the reasons why the Schools Examination and Assessment Council (SEAC), set up in 1988 to devise the testing at the Key Stages, decided upon such complex forms of assessment with different targets and levels. The trouble was that the very complexity of the testing was explicit acknowledgement that content and developmental stage do not necessarily fit well into government prescriptions. This extreme variability in development is important, however inconvenient it is for those desiring roughly uniform behaviours or competences. Furthermore it makes a mockery of school-to-school comparison, since there are massively well-documented findings linking social status to aspects of development.

Elkind writes that variation in early and middle childhood may well have something to do with the historical concept of redundancy. 'The display of variation in early childhood may be a form of redundancy, a precursor to variational displays of adolescence, which could serve as a kind of pre-selection even before adolescence' (1989, p48). He goes on to argue that an effective curriculum is one that can be tuned into at different levels and have different outcomes which are internally consistent with that particular child's needs and levels of cognition; in short, a very flexible content mediated by very careful and adapted processes of engagement.

Despite the obvious strength and appeal of the 'back-to-the-basics' movement over the last two decades, and the fact that some of these have been coupled with attempts to de-skill teachers and to control any display of intellectual independence by the profession, educational writers and researchers have made it very clear that curricula for young children are best designed from a sound developmental perspective. The NAEYC position statement is a far-reaching and carefully worded paper which was adopted by two powerful groups of early childhood educators in the USA in late 1990. The European Community document on early childhood education (Commission of European Communities, 1980) is, in many respects, not dissimilarly worded. Both have been the result of sifting ideologies, theories and research over many years. Like the Australian Schools Council document, they see the divorce of content from process as dangerous and limiting to the imagination, creativity and scope of the education systems.

Motivation and self-initiated learning

Since the middle to late 1980s there has been a body of articulate and thoroughly careful educational writers and researchers (largely, but not exclusively, in North America) making it very clear that curricula for young children are best designed from a clearly developmental perspective. They have pointed out what teachers of young children know, and perhaps feel, rather than express publicly. This is that self-initiated learning is often the key (note, *not* the Key Stage!) to any thorough capitalisation on the child's potential. Such writers have emphasised that challenge and variation are vital features, that growth is holistic and involves a mixture of the cognitive, social, physical and emotional in ways that do not easily reflect well in externally conceived packages of testable skills (Bloom, 1988; Bredekamp, 1987; Weikart, 1987). Moreover, it is probably true to say that most pre-pubertal children are still very adult-oriented and want to please their teachers. Those who are disappointed, turned off, diminished, perhaps represented as 'failures' in some tangible way quickly learn to withdraw from those challenges at school and learn to find validation in other ways. Powerful social learning may then begin to lay down patterns of behaviour which are inimical to any later scholastic success and which lead the child to find solace in the alternative peer groups of secondary school days. This is not a simple case of praising where praise is not due. It is a recognition of the central business of process-oriented education, the use of an appropriate language of encouragement.

> 'Dreikurs and Cassel (1972) state that the language of encouragement recognises the growth and contributions that students make and promotes within them self-reliance, self-direction and co-operation. The use of the language of encouragement implies that students are good enough as they are, rather than as teachers wish them to be . . . (and) all of us as teachers have a choice regarding how we will educate our students. We can control them through the use of behavioral engineering as dogs are trained and consequently make them dependent upon us, or we can nurture and encourage them to become who they can be. Ultimately the bottom line is found through the thoughtful answers to the questions, what is the purpose of education and what should students become?' (Madden, 1988, pp145–146).

None of this would surprise the majority of Infant and Junior school teachers in our schools; nor those concerned with the earlier years of education in Canada and the USA. The older ones might point to the British Plowden Report (CACE, 1967), or to the writings of Dewey and no doubt remark that much of their initial training and subsequent professional development courses, together with their own experience, would lead inevitably to conclusions emphasising developmentally based practice and sensitive language of encouragement.

The quick fix and the British disease

Why then is the British Education Reform Act (1988) so seemingly out of step with professional and research knowledge? Why, too, are there so many politicians (and newspaper columnists, Canadian and British) so anxious for a 'quick fix', or a return to what they fondly imagine were the good old days? There seem to be three main reasons for this.

Firstly, there is an undoubted residue of something akin to socially derived (or social class) attitudes to education lying deep within large sections of the populace. How this manifests itself is not simply unidirectional or consistent. It can surface in fear/dislike/mistrust of teachers and of things to do with school (an attitude still all too often stereotypically displayed by certain blue-collar groups). It can arise in the assumptions that independent, fee-paying schools are regulated by 'market forces', and that such schools of the middle and upper classes are thus exempt from the taint of ordinary persons and may eventually provide a Mafia-like network of useful contacts! It can arise in the extreme contempt shown by some politicians for the views of the profession, the attempts to largely disenfranchise them from involvement in the control of education (which led in Britain even to the removal of parent-teachers from school governing bodies). Whatever it is, one thing is quite certain; one can still discern the bones of our social class structures in public schooling (especially in England and some parts of the USA), since the very buildings are often such that, if the Factory Acts applied, they would be condemned as unsuitable, and rebuilt.

Secondly, there is a crudely *contingent* view of education prevailing in many Western societies and it dominates much of the discussion of its aims and purposes. Schooling, we are told, is to get you somewhere, preferably profitable. It is about the good society (ie the competitive, economically stable one where workers are flexible, well-matched to changing demands, and so on). Whilst all societies have to recognise that they socialise their young into some sort of 'goodness of fit' with the political and economic direction deemed desirable, many have been at pains to place the quality of the culture and its aesthetic and social concerns firmly on the agenda too. This latter aspect of education's purposes is rarely heard in England today. Indeed, we have heard it expressed only outside our shores of late (in Northern Alberta) as 'We are not just about getting our kids jobs, we are about the whole value of our culture'. Such a view is regarded as rather odd in England, though not in Europe. We are exhorted to pay attention to the world of work, both in the British National Curriculum and in the documents concerned with Initial Teacher Training (DES, 1989). Rarely are we asked to devote more time to aesthetic awareness, music, sociology, philosophy. It often appears that some of the core of the current curriculum is somewhat short-term. The assumption is that content is what matters; and this is occasionally a content of mind-boggling utilitarianism; or if not that, a content full of prejudices about what should be learned and how it should be done (witness the entirely artificial debate about phonics versus whole language. Our experience is that most early years teachers use and adapt both 'methods' anyway!)

Thirdly, a deep distrust of 'experts' in education, particularly that group which it pleases politicians to call the educational 'establishment' (professors of education, curriculum consultants, inspectors, teacher-trainers, and so on). This seems to have led to a deliberate disenfranchising of their opinions by many of the politicians. Indeed there is a tendency to talk of the 'real world of work' as outside school as if what teachers do is not work. More, currently in Britain there has been a marked tendency to ensure that committees, commissions, advisory bodies are chaired or dominated by the views of industrialists, as though this somehow gives edge or validity to the findings in a way which could not be ensured if mere educationists spoke. One is tempted to say that if schools (or indeed initial Training Institutions) were run as badly as have been those business establishments we are so often urged to emulate, then the nation's children would be in a far worse plight! Unlike the recent thorough and careful consultation going on in the wake of the Sullivan Commission (1988) in British Columbia, those peripherally involved in consultations in England have frequently been dismayed by the disregard of the profession's views. At times it seems as though even Her Majesty's Inspectors of Schools are regarded by politicians as partial or guilty of special pleading. It is hard to think of any other profession in comparable situations. Would the medical profession be allowed virtually no input into discussions on In-Vitro Fertilisation (IVF)? Such a thought is preposterous. Yet the views of teachers and their trainers are often dismissed as though they constituted some particularly obnoxious form of special pleading. Even the debate about history in the National Curriculum seemed (in 1991) to have been resolved by an arbitrary and unargued assertion as to 'where history stops' by a single politician (the then British Secretary of State).

Much of this complex arena can be reduced to one major feature; a strong belief in the country that teaching is, at best, a semi-skilled operation and, that as *operatives*, teachers should simply be instructed to 'deliver' the right content! This can then be appropriately checked if we test the children severely enough! Many would argue, indeed, that they are not a true profession.

This chapter has not set out to argue that content or assessment are not important. It may be that, after the 1944 Education Act in England, there was too much reliance on old-style incrementalism and local whim (and sometimes the extreme far-sightedness) of local education authorities. But centrally defined curriculum content has not ameliorated the differences between local education authorities. Nor has it lessened the difference between the 'good' or 'bad' school.

It is worth recalling the words of Theodore Sizer, sometime Dean at Harvard University and a noted educationist. He maintained that elementary (primary) schools do not knock up against the dole queue and the profession. They can therefore afford to have a considerably less contingent view of education. Creativity, happiness and serendipity should be found there; both the 'measured and unmeasured curriculum', as Berman (1988) called it. Defining content without leaving room for different outcomes, different processes and differing attention to the wide variability of children is a disastrous way to promote education. Narrow views of content lead to overtesting, failure and diminished self-esteem. They lead to a view of education which ignores the reality of research on children and on the transaction itself. Defined content and normative testing are simply not enough. *They lead to a mentality which concerns itself with weighing pigs, rather than properly fattening them.*

6

INTEGRATION AND THE NATIONAL CURRICULUM

As a result of the form of the National Curriculum it would be easy to see curriculum co-ordination simply in terms of specialist strength in a particular 'subject'. This chapter will argue that it is a mistake to view curriculum leadership only from the perspective of National Curriculum subject areas. The National Curriculum Council itself recognises the importance of cross-curricular provision in its definitions of cross-curricular dimensions, themes, and skills. And the various curriculum documents so far produced also encourage primary schools to think of a 'linked' curriculum. However we suggest that the focus for curriculum planning in primary schools should not be so much on integrating subject knowledge as on integrating the learning experiences of pupils. Thinking about 'principles of procedure' is one way in which the notion of curriculum leadership can be put into practice so that the emphasis is on whole curriculum planning.

Over the last thirty or so years there has been a radical shift in official thinking about the primary curriculum. The opening lines of two major government reports provide evidence of this. The 1967 Plowden Report on primary school education, *Children and Their Primary Schools*, opened with the words 'At the heart of every educational process lies the child' (CACE, 1967). By 1981, the DES in its pamphlet *The School Curriculum* offered what appears to be a deliberate alternative 'The school curriculum is at the heart of education' (DES, 1981).

In the post-war period the guiding assumption in relation to curriculum planning was that the primary curriculum should differ according to the ability and interests of the child who would follow it, and since teachers were in the best position to be informed about the ability and interests of children they should be the ones to make decisions about curriculum content. Now the creation of a National Curriculum with 'targets of attainment' at 7 and 11 denies that assumption.

Twenty years ago it was possible for a former HMI to assert that 'to young children the world is one . . . They run from one part of the field of experience to another quite regardless of the fences we put round them called subjects. They do not regard them because they do not see them, and if we insist on recognition we simply impede their progress and retard their learning' (Griffin-Beale, 1979). Now the insistence that children 'see' subjects appears to be enshrined in the presentation and organisation of the National Curriculum. So a key issue is how to combine in practice two seemingly opposing goals: the primary tradition rooted in child-centredness and individual response, with the 'rigour' demanded in an era of standardisation through a National Curriculum and its connected assessment.

Integration in the National Curriculum

The National Curriculum is organised on a subject basis, but advice from the DfE, NCC and SEAC in numerous documents is that primary school teaching should still continue to cross subject boundaries. It is instructive to document the extent to which this encouragement to integrate subject teaching at primary level occurs in the various documents. For instance, *Curriculum Guidance 1: A Framework for the Primary Curriculum* (National Curriculum Council, 1989) contains the following statements.

> The description of the National Curriculum in terms of foundation subjects is not a description of how the school day should be organised or the curriculum delivered. (Paragraph 1.1)

> The National Curriculum is not a straitjacket. It provides for greater clarity and precision about what should be taught while enabling schools to retain flexibility about how they organise their teaching. The planning of frameworks or approaches to the curriculum should be flexible enough to allow for a range of approaches to the planning of the whole curriculum and the organisation of teaching and learning in primary schools. (Paragraph 1.2)

> The National Curriculum Council recognises that in primary schools a range of work takes place which is described as 'thematic', or 'topic-based' or 'cross-curricular' in nature. It would be counter-productive to

lose existing good practice and unhelpful for the learner to devise an unnecessarily fragmented curriculum ... Planning under subject headings does not preclude flexibility of delivery across subject boundaries. (Paragraph 2.12).

The National Curriculum Council Curriculum Guidance number 3, 1990, offers a reminder that:

> Primary schools organise the delivery of the curriculum in a variety of ways ... This will include cross-curricular aspects and consideration of the ways in which a particular task may contribute to achieving several targets.

And this document also points out that: 'The programmes of study for National Curriculum subjects provide many opportunities for planning effective topic work.' NCC *Non-statutory Guidance for Science* contains a detailed example of a topic activity 'Making and Investigating a Windmill' which could form part of a topic on 'Moving Toys' at Key Stage 1. Related work in English and mathematics is provided and links that could be made with other curriculum areas are suggested – for example creating musical effects that evoke either the wind or circular movements.

All the subject documents, too, emphasise the importance of organising contexts for children's learning that cross subject boundaries. They all imply that it is possible to work through themes and topics in a way which reflects the cohesiveness that children bring to their learning at the same time as meeting the demands of the National Curriculum:

> For younger children the integration of science across the curriculum may well be the preferred way of working.
> (DES, *Science for ages 5 to 16*, 8.7)

> [In technology] we are dealing with an activity which goes across the curriculum, drawing on and linking with a wide range of subjects.
> (DES, *The Design and Technology Working Group Report*, 1.8)

> A thematic approach to the primary curriculum can help to encourage the use of mathematics in a wide range of contexts.
> (DES, *Mathematics for ages 5 to 16*, 10.35)

> Geography provides a natural context for the development of those skills identified as central to the study of English ... Many key ideas are shared by geography and mathematics ... There are certain shared interests with history .. We hope the National Curriculum in geography will stimulate the use of painting, photography, poetry, dance and drama.
> (DES, *Geography for ages 5 to 16*, 7.3, 7.6, 7.16, 7.20)

The cross-curricular process is two-way: the subject of history can benefit from the insights, knowledge and methods of other subjects, just as it can, and should, contribute to them.

(DES, *History for ages 5 to 16*, 11.1)

In primary schools the programmes of study for various subjects will interact naturally with each other.

(DES, *English for ages 5 to 16*, 8.27)

Other examples could be listed, from the Physical Education and Art documents for instance, but the statements above should be sufficient evidence that, though the National Curriculum is described in subject terms, it is possible, indeed it is recommended, that at primary level there should be a cross-curricular focus.

Planning for development

Perhaps though a concentration on integrating the different subject areas is less important than primary schools have traditionally supposed. Or rather perhaps it is less important than the process through which children acquire the knowledge element of the National Curriculum. Primary education in England and Wales has always had an emphasis on method rather than objectives and we see no reason to suggest that the strength of this approach should be weakened by the National Curriculum. Primary teachers can still concentrate on education as a process, to concern themselves primarily with the growth and development of the child so that what is learnt is fully learnt and becomes part of the intellectual and cognitive development of the learner rather than merely what the Hadow Report on primary education (Board of Education, 1931) criticised a long time ago as 'knowledge to be acquired and facts to be stored'.

It is still possible to see the prime curriculum question in terms of the developmental processes which the curriculum should promote and the kinds of methods and approaches to teaching which will enhance these processes. It is still possible to emphasise what children learn *through* a subject rather than what they must, under National Curriculum requirements, learn *of* it. As Kelly (1986) has pointed out it is not the kinds of knowledge we offer that is the crucial concern in curriculum planning, but the kinds of engagement with knowledge which we promote. Content, as Charity James (1968) has said, is an element in planning not a ground plan.

So we want to suggest that the focus for curriculum planning in primary schools should not be so much on integrating subject knowledge as on integrating the learning experiences of pupils. In this sense integrating the curriculum means ensuring that teaching and learning are coherent and integrated across subjects, so that learning is seen as a coherent whole. If curriculum leaders focused their efforts on this area there can be little doubt that pupils would reap the benefit in terms of the quality of the learning experiences they would be offered. Curriculum Guidance 3 (National Curriculum Council, 1990) makes the point that this is in fact a major responsibility: 'The Education Reform Act does not prescribe how pupils should be taught. It is the birthright of the teaching profession, and must remain so, to decide on the best and most appropriate means of imparting education to pupils'.

The National Curriculum has determined subject content, but it must be for the staff of a school to teach that content in a way which promotes learning which is active not inert (Whitehead, 1932) and is conducive to intellectual and cognitive growth rather than mere acquisition of facts.

It is our contention that providing an integrated curriculum means concentrating on the learning opportunities offered to pupils in order that they should have a continuity of experience; so that they are not seen as passive recipients of attainment target knowledge shared out to them as if they were empty vessels to be filled, but as individuals actively involved in the learning process in a way which allows their learning to become important and real for them. This means a broader, more comprehensive notion of what is involved in curriculum planning.

What we intend, therefore, in using the term 'integrated curriculum' is not an exploration of ways in which National Curriculum subjects might be put together as is most often the case in discussion of curriculum integration. Rather we prefer to pay attention to how learning can be integrated, how a unity of understanding and a coherence of experience can be developed in the minds of pupils. We see the subjects of the National Curriculum not as knowledge that has to be somehow transferred into the consciousness of pupils, but instead as media for the development of children's intellectual and cognitive abilities. Subjects can be regarded as tools of enquiry and not just as bodies of knowledge.

ACTIVITY 6.1

A question for self-reflection or staff discussion:
How do you and your colleagues encourage children to take learning seriously by letting them see that you are as concerned with their way of working as with the answer they finally come up with, that process is not less important than product?

Curriculum in action

As a leader then, how does one help others to make a judgement about whether or not the learning opportunities which children receive are of the sort which allow their intellectual involvement? How does one decide what might be required to integrate the curriculum in our definition? One way is to judge the curriculum in terms of what Stenhouse (1975) has called 'principles of procedure'. Examples of such principles might be as follows.

Activities are worthwhile in the sense of allowing children active roles in the learning situation if

- They involve children with realia (real objects, material artefacts), and help children to develop the ability to use a variety of first-hand sources as evidence from which to develop hypotheses and draw conclusions.
- Completion of the activity may be accomplished successfully by children at several different levels of ability.
- They ask pupils to examine in a new setting an idea, an application of an intellectual process, or a current problem which has been previously studied.
- They involve pupils and teachers in intellectual risk-taking ie the risk of success or failure.
- They require pupils to rewrite, rehearse and polish their initial performance, their initial efforts.
- They give pupils a chance to share the planning, the carrying out of a plan, or the results of an activity with others.
- They allow classroom discussions in which youngsters learn to listen to each other as well as express their own views and which are open-ended in the sense that definitive answers to many questions are not found.

- They encourage in children a process of question-posing.
- They encourage children to reflect on their own learning.

(adapted from Raths, 1971 and Hanley et al, 1970)

The discussion to this point should make it clear that our view of co-ordination is not confined to the notion of a specialist strength in a particular 'subject'. We consider it a mistake to see leadership roles only in terms of National Curriculum areas. As we have pointed out the various National Curriculum documents so far produced provide scope for thinking of an integrated curriculum at the primary stage in the sense that all 'subjects' might be taught with reference to certain 'principles of procedure' taking into account, and giving priority to, the process of learning rather than simply the content alone. Staff in a primary school who designed the range of activities they offered their pupils, in all curriculum areas, in ways which attempted to meet the 'principles of procedure' listed above, would be moving a considerable way towards a curriculum which leads to that coherence of experience for learners that is our concern. And none of the principles outlined here is at odds with the National Curriculum programmes of study. Indeed a number of the documents pay specific attention to such methodologies.

For instance *Science 5–16* asks teachers to encourage the active exploration of the environment, to give children the opportunity to interact with objects and materials. It points out that direct experience with objects and events is a fruitful way of extending children's knowledge and understanding. And *Curriculum Guidance 1* (National Curriculum Council, 1989) suggests that due recognition should be given to the importance of first hand experiences and practical tasks in the acquisition and application of knowledge and skills. It is hardly controversial then to suggest that the programme of every school should be organised so that it will provide opportunity for the pupils to involve themselves with realia, and to engage in activities in actual life situations. Such experiences, with appropriate teacher support, will help children expand, revise and test whatever ideas they develop.

Nor should it be controversial to suggest that the programme of every school should be organised in a way that offers children opportunities for problem-solving, encouraging the ability to analyse, review evidence, hypothesise, make decisions etc. By itself knowledge is not enough. Teaching needs to be directed at the uses of knowledge. Problem-solving is a process through which children can learn to use their knowledge, building on skills and concepts, for themselves (Fisher, 1987). It emphasises the development of qualities like curiosity, resourcefulness, independence, tenacity and patience.

Art 5–14 (DES, 1991) contains one of the many references to this aspect of the curriculum in the programmes of study which clarify how problem-solving can be a unifying force in the curriculum:

> A characteristic of work in art is the open-endedness of the tasks in which pupils are engaged. That is not to say that there are no right or wrong answers, rather that a variety of solutions is possible. A conscious under-standing of the decision-making process in art, craft and design, together with a willingness to rely on intuition as well as reasoning, should enable pupils to approach decision-making in other areas of the curriculum with some confidence. Examples could include planning an essay in English; designing an experiment in science; designing and making in technology, solving problems in mathematics; composing in music and choreograph-ing movement sequences in physical education.
>
> (para 10.5)

Similarly the understanding that children's increasing responsibility for their own learning is important for their progress and development is clear in the National Curriculum. One of the strands running through the documents is to do with pupils being encouraged to become self-confident and self-disciplined, to set their own standards and learn to appreciate when they have attained them. Confidence comes through children being able to be in charge of their work and feel they have a role in directing and organising it. It reflects a growing pleasure and involvement in learning and has to do with children's view of themselves as learners. A school should be striving to help children say to them-selves eg 'I am a writer', 'I am a reader', 'I am a scientist', 'I am an artist' because unless you have these aims of confidence and independence then you cannot really say to yourself 'I am teaching children to read', 'I am teaching children to write' etc.

Of course the level of a child's confidence will be affected by his or her previous understanding and experience of engaging with the activity and here social relationships within the group are a significant factor: a child who may work confidently in one group may be reluctant to participate in another. Similarly in the more formal social context of the classroom a young child who may be a confident and independent learner in the home setting may need support and encouragement from the teacher to act independently in the classroom. The 'principle of procedure' here is to take a child's ideas seriously so as to ensure that as these ideas develop, and the supporting evidence for them makes sense, they become 'owned' by the child. The teacher's role is as enabler, interacting with the child, raising questions, building appropriate challenges and experiences, offering new ways of thinking, and involving children in the planning, executing, presenting and evaluating of learning experiences so that 'control' is a shared responsibility.

ACTIVITY 6.2

Questions for self-reflection or staff discussion:
What forms of classroom organisation are currently used by your colleagues to encourage independent work patterns?
How can a class teacher bring together activities that the children initiate themselves and the requirements of the programmes of study?
How might your colleagues' general arrangement of areas, resources and furniture affect children's feelings of confidence and independence?
What evidence might you and your colleagues be able to gather of children's growing confidence and independence in learning?

Learning through reflection

The importance of evaluating learning experiences is often underestimated in current practice. Often, in the desire to be 'task-oriented', to 'get work done', children are not offered the time and opportunity to think about what they have done or to look together with peers or the teacher at what they have done. It is important to have an element of reflection built into the planning of curriculum activities. The ability to reflect on what has been learned is integral to children's intellectual progress. The development of reflectiveness in learning, reflective skills and the thought processes that they engender, are of central importance to cognitive development. An opportunity to think means a chance to experience a high degree of self-consciousness. A reader, for instance, may come to be more aware of his or her own response to the text, or of a writer's intentions, or may realise what this text has in common with others he or she has read. Each of these realisations would signal a growth in reflectiveness.

So the capacity to reflect consciously on what is known and on one's own thought processes, what the psychologists call meta-cognition, is an important development in learning. It is not an adjunct to education but an integral part of it at all stages, and teaching must take this into account. Again one can see evidence of this understanding in the National Curriculum. The *Science 5–16* for instance puts it like this: 'Understanding and clarifying one's own thinking is often an essential part of learning. Throughout their science education, pupils should be encouraged to develop their powers of reasoning by reflecting on their own understanding, and by appreciating that learning may involve a change in the way they think about, explain and do things', (paragraph 2.3).

ACTIVITY 6.3

Questions for self-reflection or staff discussion:
What can be done by colleagues to encourage children to review their work in a way which involves evaluating and forward planning as well as reflecting?
What opportunities do colleagues give children to have time for private reflection?
When might it be appropriate to provide such time?
How often do these periods need to occur?

It is above all through talk and discussion that the learner's capacity to reflect is developed. So, for instance, children might talk together to evaluate their evidence, or to plan the presentation of their work to different audiences in a range of ways. But this kind of activity doesn't just come at the end of a piece of work. The notion of reflection also means giving some time and space to reflecting on work in progress. Through talking about their work with other children and adults and discussing their progress in conferences with teachers, children will learn to assess their strengths and weaknesses and to think about ways in which they can become more confident and effective learners.

Of course, communication with others is an essential element of the whole learning process. All children's learning will be supported by discussion with peers and adults. Through talk children are able to make their ideas clearer to themselves as well as making them available for reflection, discussion and checking. So an emphasis on talk might be one more 'principle of procedure' that will act as an integrating factor in the curriculum. But a particular type of talk is called for: that which asks children to develop an argument, to use examples and adduce reasons, to rehearse in their own minds what others have said and assess the relevance and significance of those remarks. It would be foolish to pretend that it is easy to elicit this kind of serious conversation from children, one which encourages a co-operative search for greater understanding, with conversation passed from child to child so that children learn to value their own thoughts as well as those of others and so that they learn to subject all ideas, including their own, to careful scrutiny; but the difficulty should not be used as an excuse for avoidance, rather as an opportunity for creative consideration.

HMI have emphasised the importance of this type of discussion. In *The Curriculum from 5–16* (Department of Education and Science, 1985) for example they point out that 'talk (has) tended to be squeezed out (of the curriculum) especially that type of talk which helps young people to handle ideas, to develop a reasoned argument, to internalise experiences, and to find personal expression for them'. Attainment targets in all subjects contain reference to these kinds of skills, though not all to the same degree. For instance the Level 1 Statements of Attainment in Science suggest pupils should be able to 'describe and communicate their observations, ideally through talking in groups', in English that pupils should 'participate as speakers and listeners in group activities' and in Mathematics that pupils should 'talk about their own work and ask questions'. So, in all areas of the curriculum teachers might focus on the talk potential of each task or activity. Is it one which offers opportunity for discussion and collaboration? Can it be organised so that talk is an important dimension? For example can children be led to share their ideas by recording them on a single piece of paper rather than individually? Does the learning activity, be it a maths investigation, a CDT project, a science experiment, a piece of historical or geographical research, or the making of a story, potentially offer a challenge to children's spoken language? Intellectual involvement will come by children communicating with each other and the teacher about what they are learning, by listening, and by negotiating meanings together.

It ought to be said that if talk must be taken seriously in an integrated curriculum it is not the only way for communication to occur. There is writing of course but diagrams, sketches, plans and notation systems may often be useful, for example in recording experiments in science, developing designs in technology, devising notation systems in music, drama and dance, making illustrations in history, or using mapping systems in geography.

ACTIVITY 6.4

Questions for self-reflection or staff discussion:
What kind of questions open up children's thinking and which close it down?
What, in practice, might it mean to say that the teacher's role is to support children's learning by asking key questions and by encouragement without taking responsibility from the children?
How can time be made for the kind of conversation between a teacher and a child which helps the child to relate their work to their own life?

Working together

The National Curriculum Council's comment in Circular 3 (National Curriculum Council, 1990) that 'the aims of the National Curriculum are more likely to be achieved where . . . pupils are led to ask questions and seek answers individually and in co-operation with others' joins the idea that talk and questions should infuse the curriculum with the notion of co-operation. We would, as a final pointer towards the kinds of 'principles of procedure' that would ensure a coherent and 'integrated' curriculum want to encourage curriculum leaders to look at collaboration as a unifying force. We distinguish between co-operation and collaboration in this way: children working co-operatively might well be working individually towards some mutual end, whereas working collaboratively implies working together in such a way that the group achievement excels what might have been done by any one individual. It is integral to co-operative work that the individual will change as a result of working in this fashion, may for instance gain an insight that was not present when the group formed.

Collaborative working has many benefits. We can only hint at them here. It helps all the children in the class since the most confident children learn by displaying leadership skills while the more reluctant children gain confidence through being actively involved in an activity with others. Working in groups helps develop social skills and mutual support. It enables children to extend and modify the social strategies they use, helping a group to complete a task by referring back to what has already been discovered, by shifting the discussion forward or by building on what someone has said; supporting each other's opinions, and gaining self-esteem by having their views considered and sometimes sanctioned by the group. Collaborative working enables children to take on different roles within a group and to contribute to a shared exploration and understanding of the task. And collaborative activities with English-speaking peers give bilingual children particular support for their learning of English.

ACTIVITY 6.5

Questions for self-reflection or staff discussion:
What are the advantages of organising children to work together?
What problems might have to be overcome?
How would you support children who find it difficult to work in groups?
What are the consequences of different organisational approaches to groupings in supporting children's development?
How can you help improve the quality of group discussion between children, especially the way they listen to each other?

The business of teachers familiarising themselves with the National Curriculum system is still, no doubt, in its early stages and over the next few years schools' INSET plans will need to consider various aspects of school whole curriculum policy in the light of national requirements. In doing this we would want to recommend that schools keep in mind a statement made at the beginning of this chapter: only through children's active engagement in their own learning can what they learn be important and real for them. Primary schools ought to develop an approach to curriculum organisation which, in implementing the National Curriculum, takes this into account. We have outlined some of the areas of crucial importance if children are to be actively engaged in their own learning and encouraged to make genuine intellectual progress, so that they see the curriculum in an integrated way – procedures to do with realia, confidence and independence, problem-solving, reflection, collaboration and talk. Is there any reason why curriculum leadership should not be thought of in terms of such areas?

7

CURRICULUM EVALUATION AS REVIEW AND DEVELOPMENT: CREATING A COMMUNITY OF ENQUIRY

This chapter considers the curriculum leader's role in review and development. We explore the notion of review and development as an evaluative process integral to curriculum planning and renewal. Checks on implementation of curriculum changes are essential if curriculum leadership is to be successful. Any school needs to ask itself 'How do we know how well we are doing?' Practical suggestions are offered in relation to questions such as: How does one plan for curriculum review and development? How does one collect and make sense of the evidence in the review procedure? What is the appropriate role of the curriculum leader in this process? Relationships among staff are crucial if the review and development procedure is to work properly. We suggest that a curriculum leader's prime task in the evaluation process is the creation of an atmosphere of mutual trust and support, so that curriculum planning and renewal is done within a community of enquiry.

Evaluation, in various forms, has been working its way to the top of the educational agenda for some time now, and we have considered the use of pupil 'assessment', a restricted version of evaluation, in Chapter Five. Political reality and the climate of opinion about education means that external evaluation, via local and HMI inspections and, less explicitly, via general perceptions of the success of a school on the part of parents, LEA advisers, teachers in other schools etc, will continue to be part of educational life. It appears at the present time at least, that external evaluation is the kind that has credibility outside the profession.

National Curriculum testing has external accountability as at least part of its rationale. Yet this is all the more reason why schools should, in this climate, prove themselves capable of conducting self-evaluation and acting on the results. We consider that self-evaluation is an integral part of good teaching and should continue to be at the heart of all forms of evaluation (see Chapter Three). The concept of professionalism implies a responsibility to continuously update knowledge and skills in a striving for improvement. Teachers who view themselves as professionals will want to improve their professional practice through processes of monitoring and review. Curriculum leaders will be expected to take a lead in this process.

Central to evaluation procedures in primary schools are curriculum review and development. In practice it is impossible to separate out review and development of the curriculum from consideration of other aspects of school life such as relationships between teachers and children, teachers' professional competence and attitudes, school ethos, and importantly, children's progress and achievements. However, the discussion and activities in this chapter aim specifically to consider the curriculum as the starting point for a school's self-evaluation.

In the 1990s curriculum evaluation will have to take place against the background of the National Curriculum. Contrary to popular opinion the National Curriculum does not make curriculum planning and evaluation on an individual school basis redundant. For instance the English Statutory Orders and non-statutory guidance do not provide any detailed policies in respect to reading. Should your school continue to use reading schemes? At what point in their reading development should children be encouraged to make sensible choices about their own reading materials? Individual schools will have to continue to work out policies in these as in many other areas. So even if we accept that the National Curriculum places some restraints on the freedom of teachers to choose materials and objectives, there is still a considerable latitude within which they can make independent judgements with regard to the learning experiences they offer the children in their classroom and the ways in which these are evaluated.

Participatory evaluation: towards a synthesis of individual and school development

One of the major themes of this book has to do with collegiality and the management 'climate' of a school. Deputies and other curriculum leaders can act most effectively as catalysts in relation to curriculum evaluation and development if there is this sense of collegiality. Both theory and practice suggest that the style of leadership and management from the Headteacher will be crucial in a primary school both for the form any evaluation takes and for the commitment of the staff to it. Participatory self-evaluation inevitably requires a participatory management style (see Chapter Two). In other words if self-evaluation is going to work properly in any primary school it has to be done by, and for, members of staff, rather than to them.

Let us try to be more precise about exactly what we mean by the notion of internal, participatory curriculum review and development. Holly and Southworth (1989) offer a description which could apply to the business of curriculum review and development. They say that it is, at best, ' a learning journey based on staff involvement and focusing on classroom processes'. They suggest it is a matter of 'orchestrating and managing the change process, providing a framework for development' and 'establishing a collaborative support partnership'.

Every teacher probably carries out curriculum review as a regular but informal appraisal of the success of her own work. This process is, however, likely to be unsystematic and usually based on impressions and personal experiences without taking explicit account of information from, for instance, colleagues or pupils. Evaluation of the sort defined by Holly and Southworth implies that teachers should be prepared to think about their own practice in such a way as to enable them to make detailed judgements about that practice to themselves, but also that teachers who are moving through the change process must be supported by an institutional framework rather than working on their own (the culture of individualism described in Chapter One). In other words curriculum review, development and evaluation of the sort we would wish to recommend is neither classroom self-evaluation (which sometimes includes action research), nor school self-evaluation (which has in the past normally been to do with institutional review according to an LEA 'booklet' or 'guidelines'), nor school-based review following process guidelines such as those developed by the GRIDS – Guidelines for Review and Internal Development in Schools – project (Schools Curriculum Development Committee, 1984). Rather it is a synthesis of these activities. The whole staff look at the whole school so that everyone feels equally involved and committed to the review, but the focus is on the curriculum in individual classrooms. The aim is to combine staff ownership of the programme of review and development with a commitment to the improvement of classroom practices throughout the whole school.

Holly, Reid and Hopkins (1987) call this 'the democracy of discomfiture' and offer an example of change in one primary school where

> the staff identified music as a topic for specific review and development. The development work that has resulted from the review has included a school-based in-service course for teachers, recorder lessons being introduced in each class, an increase in the general musical activity in the school, and a determination on the part of the staff that each child should be musically literate by the time he/she leaves the school. A considerable change from a year ago when music for the majority of the pupils meant a sing-along session for half an hour each week.

The same authors quote a primary school teacher reflecting on the satisfaction she derived from being involved in this kind of activity.

> I don't mind (giving up) time because I feel that as a staff we are moving forward and an important area of the curriculum is being tackled and hopefully in the future children will benefit . . . (the process) is compelling teachers to reflect and come up with answers to such questions as 'Why am I teaching that?', 'Should I be?', 'Is it effective?', and, hopefully, 'What is best for the children?'

The kinds of activities that this teacher quoted might have engaged in may well have included such things as

- 'open house' classrooms where teachers can openly visit each other as a basis for later discussion
- staff workshops which concentrate on the practicalities of organising learning in the classroom
- paired observation with a 'critical friend' leading to the formation of relevant issues which are fed into staff discussions.

Asking staff to observe in each other's classrooms may at first appear impractical and idealistic, but as Little (1981) points out there *are* schools where 'classroom observation is so frequent, so intellectually lively and intense, so thoroughly integrated into the daily work, and so associated with accomplishments for all who participate that it is difficult to see how the practices could fail to improve teaching'.

One final point needs to be made before some suggestions for a practical programme of review and development are offered. Resources and time are obviously inhibiting factors in any attempt at curriculum review. It is important that the workload of the review matches the availability of people to take it on and a timetable is drawn up which involves minimum disruption. In a primary school it is almost inevitable for example that meetings between staff will have to take place outside 'teaching time', but it is most important that the suggestions that follow are not seen simply as 'bolt-on' activities. By combining various approaches to the review process, it ought to be possible to provide a framework which becomes integrated into the ongoing work of the school rather than an extra burden. The general principle is that for curriculum review and development to work it must be absorbed into current practice, integral to the organisation of learning, not an optional extra. In other words, if curriculum review and development is to become important in any school it must take root in the institution itself, rather than be seen as just one more administrative feature of school life. Clift, Nuttall and McCormick (1987) suggest that 'in its idealised form school self-evaluation requires idealised schools in which collegiality, co-operation, open communication and fraternity rule (to say nothing of sorority) and where professional development and professional respect go hand in hand.'

Curriculum review and development: planning for action

It may be that your school has a history of considerable professional development in relationship to the part of the curriculum now under review. It might therefore be helpful to draw a concise picture of the history of work in this area in recent years. Perhaps draw a time line on a large sheet of paper and then discuss with colleagues all the external and internal INSET activities that have been of relevance over the last five years and mark them on your time line. You should include any developments that involved the whole staff and also, if individuals are willing to identify their involvement in particular groups or courses, personal aspects of the overall picture. This time line will give you some idea of the staff's overall awareness of developments in the teaching of the area under review as well as each member's knowledge and experience. Although the National Curriculum may still be dominating thinking in your school it would be wrong not to clearly acknowledge staff experience and expertise not directly related to developments linked to the National Curriculum.

Although school-based curriculum review starts with the needs within the school, this does not mean that external demands and advice should be ignored. At the start of any internal review it is important to find out about recent research and other developments relevant to the aspect of the curriculum under review and to try to draw together a picture of what is generally regarded as good practice. This picture will necessarily have to take account of the National Curriculum programmes of study. What is good practice?

One might ask the staff as a group to draw up a list of all the educational initiatives, publications, projects etc that they know of that have influenced their practice in the curriculum area under review in recent years. In discussion staff knowledge can then be shared and pooled. As an alternative activity ask each member of staff to write six statements which they feel describe good practice in the area under review.

Then come together as a group to discuss each member's list. From all the statements select the nine which the group thinks are the most important and use these statements as a basis for discussing current practice in the school.

Thinking about change

As much of this book implies, bringing about change demands changes of attitude as well as changes of teaching practice. This is a sensitive area and it is essential to select strategies for change that will suit both the curriculum leader and the rest of the staff (see Chapter Three). Formal staff meetings are not always the best means by which to effect change.

There are a range of strategies that might be used to support curriculum review and development. There are those which involve work in school. These might include for instance

- staff/curriculum meetings
- INSET days
- INSET packs and videos
- observation of children working
- sharing children's work
- questionnaires and other forms on information gathering
- workshops
- sharing with colleagues the planning of project work
- working alongside or team-teaching with colleagues.

This last is important. Teachers rarely see other teachers at work and therefore have only hazy notions against which to judge their own teaching. Working in another classroom inevitably involves observation and perhaps consequent nervousness, but if a teacher 'under observation' today is 'observer' in another classroom tomorrow a collaborative atmosphere should be engendered where all value visiting each other's classrooms and accept its consequences. In particular 'paired teaching' can be a good way of influencing others and implementing curriculum policies.

A large part of the task of a curriculum leader is about influencing colleagues. This is an activity fraught with difficulties, but enlisting a colleague's support in a joint venture of some kind avoids accusations of exceeding authority and engenders a commitment to the proposal. The least threatening elements in any review are inanimate objects such as curriculum materials and resources and it may well be that these aspects constitute a suitable point of commencement for teachers unused to the notion of curriculum review. In any case two 'points of procedure' in any joint venture would have to be friendship and voluntaryism.

Consider also strategies which use external support, and which might provide a new and fresh perspective. These might include:

- visits to other schools
- ideas from self-help groups and networks
- visits to exhibitions, courses, lectures etc at professional development centres and universities
- support from advisers and advisory teachers
- attendance at local association meetings.

Making a plan

It may be better to concentrate on one particular aspect of the curriculum at a time than to try to advance on all fronts at once. Planning that is over-ambitious may only serve to irritate and demoralise staff. Prioritising is vital. A few aspects of the curriculum might be reviewed in depth each year, but this within a cyclic approach. Planning means deciding what you intend to do and how you intend to do it. In the context of curriculum review of the sort we have been discussing there must be a personal and group contract however informally agreed to get things done. The process of making specific planning statements can also be useful in ensuring group consensus. Perhaps make sure that the staff are in agreement on the following issues before starting the review process:

- Do all involved in the process share a common understanding of the parameters of the review? For example, if the review is to do with spelling, do you intend that discussion and activities should spill over into general policies to do with writing?
- Do you agree that all staff should participate, even in a large school, or, for example, is this a review for a particular year group?
- What time scale is to be allocated?
- Do you agree about who is to take the major initiatives in leading the review and development process? Is it the Headteacher, the Deputy, another curriculum leader, or should it be a small working party?

The model below suggests one possible approach to developing a review and developmental plan, but it is by no means definitive. Although the model is systematic, you will need to adapt the approach to your particular circumstances. Any review will reflect previous work done in the area, the level of knowledge and expertise amongst the staff, the requirements of the National Curriculum, and the opinions of parents and governors, amongst other factors. Our procedure is based on a model developed by Coles and Banks (1990) which in turn is freely adapted from a model for developing a school assessment policy produced by the Primary School Assessment Project (Hants LEA with Southampton University, 1989). That project's procedures have been redesigned so that our model has six elements which together form the acronym ADRENALIN.

1. Analyse
2. Decide and
   Review
3. Establish what you are going to do and
   Note your action plan
4. Advise colleagues and
   Let people know what is happening
5. Implement
6. Now evaluate

Each element involves asking a question, agreeing a task and engaging in a number of activities with a specific result in mind.

Analyse
Question: What is the school's current practice?
   Task: To review and analyse existing practice.
   Activities: If any review is to be rigorous it must have some degree of objectivity, and objectivity requires the use of evidence. It does not though necessarily mean 'from the outside'. Below are brief summary statements of the type of activity it would be useful to undertake in order to collect evidence.

- Ask each teacher to summarise on one side of A4 paper her practice in the area under consideration. Circulate these sheets among the staff prior to a whole staff discussion.

- Send out a brief questionnaire to all staff asking relevant questions about existing practice. Again, circulate responses in preparation for a staff discussion. Questionnaires are economic in terms of time but they are not as easy to design as might first appear. Keep it short, make it easy to respond to, make it easy to return the form.

- Collect relevant examples of children's work which demonstrate current practice, and bring them to the staff meeting.

- Collect relevant books and other teaching materials which demonstrate current practice and bring them to a staff meeting.

- Organise a simple questionnaire for the children, to gather information about their understanding of current practice.

- In groups brainstorm the various approaches taken in different classrooms.

- Organise 'paired teaching' sessions when the curriculum area under review is being concentrated on in the classroom.

- Hold interviews with staff about their current practice. This might be threatening but can be most fruitful if findings are shared, since interviews have the advantage of allowing for follow up and clarification of response. Be aware also though that interviewing can be expensive in terms of time, because in a primary school of ordinary size, all staff would have to be interviewed to gain a fair picture. A sheet can be constructed with a set of prepared questions to assist information gathering and reporting back.

Result: A common understanding of the range of curriculum activities practised within the school.

Decide and review

Question: What shall we do to improve existing practice?

Task: To review existing practice and to agree principles related to the area under review.

Activities: Using information gathered during the previous stage, as well as ideas formed as a result of other INSET activities, identify and agree the principles and purposes which will influence your school's policy by asking teachers to ask themselves certain questions. For example:

- What needs changing?
- Identify some differences and similarities in the approaches taken by various teachers. Do the differences matter?
- Looking at National Curriculum programmes of study as well as Statements of Attainment, is the curriculum you offer falling short in any area? Remember that the root of any decisions lies in what each child is doing in the classroom and perhaps formally note decisions taken and provide each member of staff with a copy of those decisions.

Result: The establishment of some firm principles for developing existing practice which have the agreement of the whole staff.

Establish and note your action plan

Question: What approach shall we take to make any changes necessary?

Task: To produce an action plan for introducing new practice or revising existing practice.

Activities: Through discussion:

- Consider what the policy decisions mean for classroom practice.
- Agree a time scale for all innovations.
- Find out what costs and resources are involved, if any.
- Decide what monitoring procedures will be adopted.
- Determine how any changes will be evaluated.
- Identify people responsible for carrying out particular tasks.

Result: The establishment of a plan of action for carrying through some curriculum development.

Advise and let people know

Question: Who needs to know about the review and resulting proposed developments?

Task: To make formal and informal reports on the review and any changes in practice to governors, parents, and receiving schools.

Activities: Discuss the review and proposed developments with other professional colleagues, such as other local curriculum leaders, and the relevant teachers in receiving schools.

- Prepare a document detailing the agreed changes in practice for circulation amongst staff (these documents can eventually build into a file of agreed practice across the curriculum for new appointees to the school).
- Summarise the review and developments which led to the new practice in a concise statement for parents and governors. Then perhaps hold a meeting to discuss the change and explain it to parents and governors.

Result: The change is approved and agreed, perhaps with modifications. It is stated in a precise written form and made available for consultation by interested parties.

Implement

Question: How do we manage the implementation of the development stage?

Task: To support and monitor changes in practice.

Activities:

- Prepare a series of stages, identifying specific activities, and communicate this to all concerned.
- Introduce monitoring meetings which involve either 'paired' staff, or small teams or the whole staff.
- Identify one person (the curriculum leader?) who will note and document the implementation process, especially staff reactions, implications for resources, the responses of children and parents, and any emerging difficulties that become apparent.
- Continue with 'paired observation' and 'team teaching' activities, this time perhaps asking these questions:
  What did the children actually do?
  How worthwhile was it?
- Decide when the implementation stage is complete, and agree upon what evidence this decision will be based.

Result: The full introduction into the school of some new or revised classroom practice in a particular curriculum area.

Now evaluate

Question: How well is the curriculum working in practice?

   Task: To evaluate the new or revised practice.

   Activities: The activities in this section take for granted a willingness not only to plan and enact worthwhile developments in the curriculum in your school, but also to evaluate those developments and use that evaluation for future planning in the cyclical model of curriculum review and development.

- Review the notes and documentation that were gathered as part of the implementation process.
- Hold a single item staff meeting to discuss the new policy or practice focused on the question 'How well are we doing?'

   Result: An awareness of the success or failure of the change, and an opportunity to consider adjustments.

It is important to understand that *evaluation is an integral part of the review and development process*. For instance, if you assess, evaluate and carefully observe children as part of a pupil profiling procedure, some of the information you gather will help evaluate the curriculum in action. Similarly, if you have an appraisal system for staff, this gives teachers a chance to contribute to the evaluation, and to air views about change in the curriculum. So within the cycle of curriculum development it is best to see implementation and evaluation as occurring in the same phase, otherwise evaluation may occur so long after the planning and enactment of the new practice that it cannot suggest ways of improving implementation. The School Development Plans Project (DES, 1989) links implementation with evaluation, suggesting some necessary elements for a successful implementation of the innovations which follow from curriculum review (see Figure 7.1).

   Checks on implementation and success mean continually asking the question 'How well are we doing?' Curriculum review and development is rather like painting the Forth Bridge – never completed. Having discussed and agreed change and attempted to put that change into practice, evaluation of that practice will more often than not reveal other aspects of practice that require attention. The following list of questions and activities are suggestions for ways to keep this cyclical process as effective and smooth as possible.

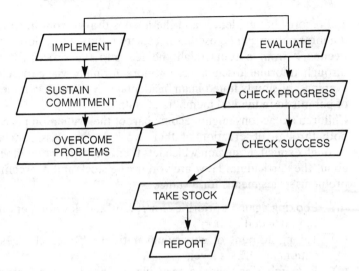

Figure 7.1

Are the staff as a team continuing to offer each other collegial support? For instance:

- Headteachers could make themselves available to discuss progress and problems with staff on a one-to-one basis.
- Teachers might find a way of letting each other know that their work in the change process is appreciated.
- Team meetings could be held to discuss progress and deal with problems. Ensuring that everyone receives regular feedback and summaries of progress can help keep up commitment and motivation.
- The school might organise informal lunchtime chats amongst staff on curriculum matters.

What checks on implementation and progress are being made? For instance:

- Each staff meeting could have a brief time set aside for reviewing progress, reflecting on the developments, noting changes that have taken place and working out the implications for future work.
- The curriculum leader might want to collect evidence of changes

and record that evidence, and the lessons drawn from it, so that the information can be used as necessary in future developments.

- Feedback from parents might be fed into the process, either through informal discussions, or more formally via curriculum evenings, or simply noted in an incidental way through comments of parents to individual members of staff.
- Children's reactions might become part of the evaluation process, both through observation of their work in the classroom and through explicit discussion which lets them express a point of view about the curriculum. How are you taking stock and overcoming problems? This means for instance:

   (a) Looking again at priorities for review and development that were decided earlier;
   (b) Taking account of curriculum initiatives/policy changes at national or LEAs level;
   (c) Remembering that the particular needs of a school change with time and taking this into account by readjustments or major rethinking;
   (d) Renegotiating the review timetable as priorities change, or if it takes longer than you expected to do things.

Finally, this section has emphasised that planning for continuing curriculum review should be part of a development policy and that a structured way of doing that is needed.

The role of the curriculum leader

So what is the role of the curriculum leader in all of this? Well, since any curriculum review may lead to proposals for major changes, skills of leadership are of the greatest importance. We have discussed this issue in Chapters One and Two but some additional points need to be made here. It has been suggested that the type of school leader needed for effective evaluation to be carried through is 'able to diffuse professional threat, engender openness and honesty, ensure participation, and carry forward reforms' (Clift et al, 1987) and that the staff climate most conducive to successful review is characterised by 'openness, trust, a preparedness to face risk and ambiguity, a positive attitude to curriculum' (Holly and Southworth, 1989). So what factors can foster these qualities? Perhaps the major factor is to do with who retains ownership of the

---

ACTIVITY 7.1

The following list of questions might be used in the curriculum review and development discussions in any school:

- How long is it since we reviewed our practice and policy in relation to this curriculum area?
- Are we still committed to our overall aims or are we inclined to alter them in some way?
- What goals have we set in the past?
- How did we decide to achieve these goals?
- What have we actually achieved?
- What have been our successes and our failures?
- What changes will we make now?
- What will be our detailed plans for the next time period in relation to this part of the curriculum?
- When will we review these plans?
- Who is the person responsible for co-ordinating and carrying forward these plans?

---

exercise. Is there a management style of reciprocity that fosters commitment to the review? One way to discover the answer to this question would be to think about the following questions, adapted from Kemp and Nathan (1989):

ACTIVITY 7.2

- Is there a clear sense among colleagues of belonging to a team?
- Does the team have a clear sense of identity as such?
- Can members of the team voice different opinions without disturbing team spirit?
- Are particular skills/expertise/qualities of team members recognised and used?
- Is there a positive attitude among all team members in relation to team tasks?
- Is the process of decision making in the team effective?
- Is there evidence that decision making involves all team members?
- Is there a pattern of properly organised meetings of the team, formal or informal as appropriate?

If staff work as a team then all should feel involved and committed to the enterprise and all should feel to some extent under review. And collaboration should also lessen the personal anxiety which any review will engender. So curriculum review and development by collaborative enquiry offers a solution to the apparently intractable situation in many primary schools where teachers remain isolated from one another behind classroom doors, where schools have an ethos that promotes isolation, so that though in most schools school-wide problems are solved together, teachers still do not discuss in any detail what they do in the classroom, or seek collegial solutions to significant classroom problems, or ensure themselves through such discussion that children are getting a genuinely consistent experience through the school.

The concept of 'critical friendship' is important here (see Chapter One). Part of a curriculum leader's role in a staff team will be to observe and facilitate, to act as a sounding board in their area of expertise, to question practice in a way which poses no threat to other individuals, or indeed to the whole school ethos. This implies, as other discussions in this book note, a move from the marginal role which curriculum postholder's traditionally have had, often doing no more than ordering resources and helping Headteachers write schemes of work, to a central role which carries genuine leadership tasks, the individual who has prime responsibility for developing the curriculum in a particular area, and working to maintain good practice in that area. So now curriculum leaders, in order that they are able to provide the impetus for curriculum review and development must keep up to date in their area of curriculum responsibility, know its conceptual structure, be able to make professional judgements about methodologies, resources and materials, represent their area of responsibility to outsiders, as well as perhaps teach alongside colleagues, lead discussions, and advise probationary teachers.

The ambiguities and complexities of engaging in these kinds of activities inevitably bring potential problems. For instance, some tension might be created if the particular area of responsibility of one teacher is seen to be operating inadequately; but this is one more reason for staff relations to be such that the overarching feeling, regardless of day to day pressures and 'hassles', is one of mutual support, sharing and professional growth. Another potential problem may be a tension between the role of the curriculum leader in curriculum review and development, the Headteacher's curriculum role, and some teachers' desire for autonomy in the classroom. The various roles of the curriculum leader have been discussed at length in Part One. Suffice it to say here that possible areas of conflict might be anticipated and avoided to a large extent if members of staff have agreed amongst themselves the areas of a curriculum leader's responsibilities (through job descriptions for example) and have themselves, by sharing experience and expertise, fashioned the curriculum policy decisions which might act as a yardstick against which practice is measured.

Some time ago Skilbeck (1982) anticipated some of the expertise and social skills that might be required: 'The task is complex and difficult for all concerned. It requires cognitive skills, strong motivation . . . constructive interactions in planning groups and emotional maturity.'

ACTIVITY 7.3

The following list of questions, adapted from Biott (1991) might be used by a staff who wish to review how well they are acting as a collaborative group.

- Does the group share a language which is encouraging and supportive as well as analytical?
- Is the group using evidence for its interpretations and review which is available to all participants?
- Are all viewpoints in the evidence, including children's comments, treated equally?
- Have the enquiries led to people wanting to do things as a result?
- Is the group confident enough to welcome the participation of outsiders in its work?

ACTIVITY 7.4

Make a list of all the things you would like to do in the curriculum review and development exercise. Divide these activities into two groups: those that are part of a continuing role as a curriculum leader; and those which are specific to the review in your particular curriculum area. Think about what colleagues are doing in other curriculum areas. Does your school have specific expectations of curriculum leaders?

So the school's expectations of the curriculum leader and her role in curriculum review are crucial. Effectiveness will be increased if the

Headteacher and curriculum leader have spent time clarifying the role and responsibilities. How the curriculum leader views her role in the review and development exercise will depend on various factors, such as how recently she has taken the role on, how long she has worked at the school, and how the school is organised. Activity 7.4 will help you to reflect on your role, perhaps as a basis for negotiating a job description.

The following are some of the activities and roles you may have considered.

- Providing colleagues with information on research and developments in curriculum.
- Developing and demonstrating your own good practice.
- Sorting out resources and ordering new stock.
- Setting up displays and co-ordinating specific school activities related to your area.
- Leading discussions about the curriculum.
- Co-ordinating record-keeping and assessment.
- Providing support and advice to colleagues.
- Acting as a 'critical friend'.
- Co-ordinating liaison with other schools.
- Looking at ways of involving parents and keeping them informed of developments.
- Spreading enthusiasm for the area of your expertise amongst other staff.
- Paired observation projects.
- Keeping in touch with local and national developments in your particular curriculum area.

We have emphasised, in this chapter as in others, how important it is that curriculum leaders see one of their prime tasks as the creation of an atmosphere of mutual trust and support, so that curriculum planning and renewal is done within a community of enquiry. We want also to repeat the other main theme of this chapter. The processes of monitoring and review are integral to good teaching, and this is as true at institutional level as it is at the level of the individual teacher. If a school is to be successful in terms of the quality of the learning experiences it offers its children, curriculum evaluation and development has to be integral to its work. It is a commitment to the improvement of classroom practices throughout the whole school.

8

WHAT SCHOOL IS REALLY FOR: REVISITING VALUES

This chapter focuses on the values which underlie notions of education and schooling. It takes some of the principal concerns of previous chapters: relationships, reflective leadership, developmentally based practice, responsibility; and examines them in the light of some of those past, current and (perhaps) more enduring values which provide the context for debates about the purpose of schooling and about what makes the institution effective. It is meant to remind the reader of salient issues – but is also intended to provide a coherent rationale for and overview of perspectives of learning. These perspectives remind us of the centrality of the child in it all.

Any final chapter in a book concerned with issues which preoccupy those one might term 'middle managers' should of necessity throw certain fundamental, recurring problems into relief. The prime one of these is that of achieving a balanced recognition by parents, teachers, governors and children that they are mutually interdependent in the exercise, that they must all know what school is really about, what it can be expected to achieve and what not. We must be careful about the wholesale adoption of the language of industry and commerce, since much is highly damaging to education and may subtly distort and misrepresent the processes, perhaps especially so at the levels of early childhood and primary education. For in the 1990s the language of education has been thoroughly taken over by the jargon of the market place. Courses are 'delivered'; the quality of teaching is 'controlled'; there are enterprise

'initiatives' which make learning and creativity seem subservient to efficiency or 'standards'. Children are defined as 'products'. Schools and
classes have 'outcomes'; teaching skills and subtleties are defined as
'competencies' to be defined on the job and rarely to be reflected upon
in any professional manner! In particular, pedagogical theory is derided
and effective teacher training thought to consist of solely practice, with
as little reflection or theory as possible.

The curriculum writer Berman has pointed to the danger of such
language usage, saying, 'Within such a framework (of thinking) the
products of education can be easily considered in quantifiable scores and
the language of education becomes that of numbers' (Berman, 1987,
p346). Thus, whilst we must as childhood educators be cognisant with
the current vogue for images of accountability and product 'quality
control' borrowed from industry (including the near deification of 'market forces' approaches to schooling), we must seek constantly to debate
and emphasise other more important features.

Schooling and education are, of course, not necessarily synonymous.
Education, one hopes, is a life-long process of humanising and developing. Schooling is relatively short and, parents assume, reasonably systematic. We should remember too that many adolescents escape
thankfully from school to an outside world often more meaningful and
more stimulating. Moreover, we should remember the relative *position*
of school in the scheme of socialisation and the acquisition of values (see
Figure 8.1), since we know from a variety of surveys that, for instance,
other influences, such as television, are nowadays of paramount importance and may well preoccupy even the three-year-old for as much as
twenty hours per week. Not only is it easy for us to confuse education
and schooling it is just as easy to confuse certification with it all. We may
think that the measures of achievement add up to something altogether
more significant than they really do, to think that marks and diplomas
gained somehow equal the education itself! True they may overlap, but
they are often painfully – almost irrelevantly – distinct.

Schools work in the real world, within the context of values expressed
by or implicit in parents' and society's actions, critically mediated by the
impressions and images of the consumer society. Such contexts may well
generate messages of greater meaning for children than can school; and
frequently those messages are presented in packages of such sophistication, attractiveness and slickness, that no mere schoolteacher can easily
counter the fashion or the thought.

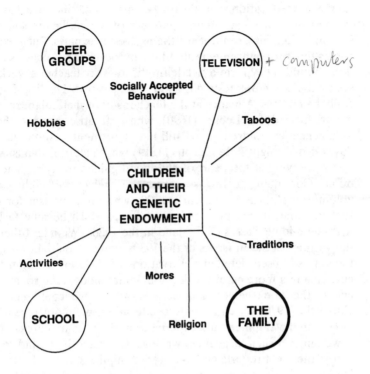

Figure 8.1   Influences on the growing child

As 'leaders' at home and at school parents and teachers need to recognise the power of modern advertising, of images of great salience being available at the touch of a button. They need to be aware that there are many factors affecting the socialisation of our young. And, of course, schooling *is* about socialisation; it has to be about utility and societal 'fit', but it must leave room for freedom and creativity, for both the measured and the unmeasured curriculum.

Rhetoric and reality in educational fashion

Anyone who has been involved in education for more than ten years or so may well, at times, display a little cynicism about 'fashions' in education. Since education can always be improved, since we have all, in Western societies, had some experience of school, lay person and professional alike may well regard themselves as experts. Such experience means that pronouncements about the purposes and processes of education abound. They form a rich leitmotif to every teacher's work. Topics are in; topics are out; testing is good; testing is bad. The list of assertions could be endless. A glance at the teacher's bookshelf might reveal comments from John Locke (1690) whose treatise against the 'over-indulgence' of children would still find agreement in some quarters today. Or one might note Crispus (1814) whose stern Calvinist views on depravity lying at the heart of childhood guided many a Victorian dominie. Continuing to browse across the shelves we might stray to a volume by Holmes in the early 1900s whose enthusiasm for freedom fuelled some of the 'progressive' thoughts which became fashionable with the middle classes of England in the 1920s. We might then turn to the writings of Susan Isaacs of the 1930s; and we could, in passing, note the way she used detailed observations of children to begin to frame curricula in a more carefully developmental mode. And so, as we range across the bookshelves, almost at random, we could come across Entwistle (1970) on child-centred education, or, more recently, Blyth (1984) on development and experience in the primary curriculum. Even if we ignored such 'academic' writings, we would be bound to stumble across the great reports and ministerial enquiries, from Hadow through Butler, to Plowden, or perhaps ponder on the polemics of the Black Paper writers of the late 1960s and early 1970s, or those of Warnock or Lawlor today.

Everyone, it seems, has written about education, about its purposes, about the 'necessary' curriculum, about testing. Can you blame the class teacher, curriculum leader, Headteacher or teacher trainer for feeling just a little weary at times? All these enquiries; all these expert opinions. One can almost hear the tired response, 'Ah well, they should try it with little Mary Jones on a Friday afternoon', and so on.

If one returns to the browsing through reports and research, through opinion and legislation, one is immediately struck by the thought that *policy* does not appear logically consistent, articulated, or even particularly guided by research. Perhaps it is naive to expect the latter. One notes that belief, rather than substance, seems as much the power behind legislation for schooling (and curriculum change) as any cool rational enquiry. Indeed, our brief glance at the bookshelves of education could as well demonstrate how great changes occurred almost by whim. Worse perhaps, that powerful findings or pronouncements become overtaken by temporary need and that the latter has a more lastingly shaping effect than earlier defined intention. Did large-scale vertical grouping in British primary schools come about from conviction, or largely from the necessity of the falling rolls of the 1970s, one might ask? It is hard not to be cynical. Are we busy integrating 'special needs' children into the ordinary classroom (and closing down most special schools) only to wake up at some year in the future to find that special, focused, separate provision is once again the order of the day? (A feature already presaged in some parts of the United States.)

The history of education could so easily also be assembled in the form of a roll call of illustrious commissions and reports; most of which are now outmoded, superseded, or ignored! The Plowden Report (CACE, 1967) is currently being derided and misrepresented in some quarters of government and the media. Indeed, whereas most of those at all familiar with primary teaching are aware that the tragedy was that Plowden never sufficiently *took hold*, we are now told that an over-reliance on Plowden 'methodology' is responsible for all ills and is the root cause of this or that failure. The principles of Plowden are distorted, more especially by some branches of the press, so as to appear synonymous with the language of sloppiness or of insufficient discipline. The careful marriage between process and content is ignored or, worse, declared null and void.

Recognising autonomy and responsibility

Perhaps one of the commonest 'mistakes' in thinking of schooling and the curriculum is to take the view that there is only one set of clients, the parents. If one does take such a view, then the implications for the curriculum are very serious indeed. Firstly, the parents will often have a (necessarily) rather limited and subjective view of what they want for their children. Secondly, they may well have a view, somewhat glossily enhanced by the selective processes of human memory, that is embedded in the past, that implies stasis and tradition, rather than expansion and change. Thirdly, most parents (and there is nothing intrinsically wrong with such a view) will want their children to succeed financially, or achieve status, or, perhaps, fulfil secret longings that they themselves had as children. There are other factors which must be taken into consideration. Briefly, they are as follows: the school curriculum is as much for the children *now*, as for their long-term future. It must be capable of expansion and relocation and not seen simply in terms of fixed content. It should reflect the whole society and not be simply viewed solely as the means of achieving greater economic progress. Above all, it should commit children to decisions about their part in it all. We can perhaps illustrate this best by referring to a story from the childhood of one of the authors. In the late 1940s at about the age of ten years he began attending the Oxford High School for Boys; a school now defunct, but housed in a particularly fine building designed by Jackson. To his juvenile mind the school seemed immensely large; it wasn't; it held about five hundred boys. The teachers (masters) seemed very old. He has since realised that they weren't, either! One meeting with the senior master, Mr R W Bodey, made a lasting impression. The new boys were gathered together to hear what science was about and how our curriculum should proceed. Mr Bodey stood before us and said something like this. 'My object gentlemen, is not so much to teach you physics, as to bring you up as good Christian citizens, you worms. My views on education may not interest you, but they focus my attention and behaviour such that I intend you learn responsibility; responsibility for your thoughts and actions, but above all [and I fancy his voice softened] responsibility for each other; that is what education is about.' Mr Bodey is now dead, but his words, or the author's half-recalled approximation of them, have stayed with that author for half a century. Incidentally, he rarely if ever had a 'failure', since he taught science with a mixture of humour and enquiry which would still be the envy of many.

Mr Bodey's view of the curriculum was not one which would have easily fitted into the current ten subjects of the National Curriculum. It *might* conceivably be partly encompassed by the 'cross-curricular themes', or something like Personal and Social Education. But primarily it was about recognising autonomy and responsibility, about causal attributions both in the self and within the scientific method. For Mr Bodey I believe that the object of a good curriculum at any age was not so much to achieve a given mastery of content as to achieve a given mastery *over one's person*. Autonomy was a word he liked; responsibility another. Autonomy, as is pointed out in an earlier chapter, means the quality of and act of being self-governing and self-reliant (though not necessarily selfish) and most writers have thought of it in three main spheres: those of *emotions, behaviour and values*. To my mind the ideal school curriculum would not design situations in which children were expected to be passive, nor would government missives talk of its 'delivery', as though some crude parcel of knowledge was all that was required. Ideally, a curriculum values autonomy so that children can be responsible for their learning and their social behaviour from the start. In many respects, unfortunately, schools and their curricula run quite counter to this notion. They contain within them notions which can be best explained as 'not wanting children to depart from the way of truth', even if the 'truth' is a frozen mishmash of past tradition, rather than much related to current realities! Children are very much 'social products' of this time; that is they are not recreations of one's own childhood a generation earlier. As such they are much more *in* the modern world, often more aware of contemporary influences, changes in knowledge, than are their parents (or, indeed, any adults). Thus, the balance in the curriculum is something which inevitably is quite delicate. Put this way, it is apparent that no national 'fixed' curriculum could ever succeed, because, as times change, so do the relative merits of some of what should or should not be included in the programme. Is there really much point in teaching quadratic equations, for instance? Does it really matter if we leave out some of the 19th-century narrative poems (grand though they are), because we now wish to incorporate some contemporary women's poetry? Surely, the answer must be *no*. If one takes Mr Bodey's avowed intentions one could teach self-responsibility and the wish to further one's own eduation as much through coracle-weaving as through kinetic energy!

Another aspect of the curriculum which is often left out is *how it appears to children* and how they attribute their success or otherwise. What too of responsibility? Its literal meaning is 'able to be called upon as a prime cause or agent, the quality of being held accountable'. In the educational context it more often has to do with the recognition of the role of one's own effort in the educational enterprise. If only schools could realistically present ways in which this could be achieved!

A core curriculum and individual need

When talking of schooling, we should remember that there is no *single justification for even a core curriculum*. Currently, in England and Wales we follow the legislation of 1988 which provides for ten core and foundation subjects in the British National Curriculum. But there are a variety of arguments concerning core curricula, and some are complementary; some compete. At any age and stage, the types of core curricula arrived at are merely a reflection of the different emphases or criteria chosen. 'Educational Entitlements' seem to be the central components in the current British (and Australian) approaches; and we have seen from many discussions in the educational press (and from at least one official report: Alexander, Rose and Woodhead, 1992) that therein lie many tensions; most notably those between 'areas of experience' and modes of 'integration', between specialist content and looser polymathic generalism. The current British ethos is such that the 'developmentally appropriate practice' of the North American researchers is either misunderstood as an educational principle, or, worse, is deliberately misrepresented. The current *official* British position seems to be one that could be deemed content rich and process thin; a strange situation for a country until recently admired for its apparent strengths in primary education!

At the heart of much of the theory and ideology of British primary and early years education, and we must acknowledge that theory and ideology are both confused and enmeshed, lies respect for each individual in school – and respect by him or her for each and all of the others. Schools which exhibit such central values can be seen positively to thrive on diversity such that mutuality and respect for persons become a major part of what the school is really about. Kirby, like many other primary educators, said that four key ideas had dominated early childhood education generally. These were:

1. Respect for children and what they do, particularly the recognition of each child's unique, unrepeatable identity.

2. The belief that human beings are different and that it is important for the educational process to acknowledge the individual character of each person and of the qualities and distinctions that he or she brings.

3. The recognition that experience (especially social experience) is a prime feature in learning and a vehicle for interpreting the world at large.

4. An awareness that the environment is vital and not only plays a major part in making that person unique, but can be used as a major vehicle in education.

(Kirby, 1981)

Articulating the vision

For schools to be good, well-matched to the children's needs and abilities and able to function articulately in a minefield of conflicting goals represented as desirable in a modern society, no mere adherence to ill-defined and less-well-articulated principles can be enough. It is therefore especially important that teachers see themselves as professionals, able to describe, analyse and cogently place their practices in the context of research and common understandings. Unfortunately there is a tendency for many primary teachers (and Heads?) to know one hundred and one uses for old toilet rolls or plastic bottles without being able to articulate the principles that underpin their use! Professionalism means knowing, describing and defending one's views of education. It is not achieved simply through the in-group building of restrictive practices and private languages. It is much more likely to be achieved through rational argument and constant explanation, through conviction and idealism, through continued study and reflection on practice. Richard Peters was probably right when he suggested that a major contribution by early childhood educators (usually, but not always, the proponents of what are loosely termed 'child-centred' approaches) was to emphasise important principles such as autonomy and respect for persons as *the* fundamentals in deciding how schooling should proceed. But how does a school exemplify these features within its organisation and how does it justify them to the wider community? Answers to these questions are probably best culled from actual case studies of schools or from biography. But, in general, we believe it essential that leaders in primary schools should:

1. Try to establish fundamental agreement on what school is for, both with parents and among the staff: that is, recognise the very real tensions which exist between demands for utility and demands for personal fulfilment. These tensions should be discussed regularly and made *explicit*.

2. Acknowledge that *transaction frequently overrides content*: (see Chapter Five) that is that the relationship between teacher and pupil is the most important single factor in learning. This means reminding all concerned that we are dealing with pre-pubertal and (often) very adult-oriented children. It means emphasising points made in the earlier chapters, ie that definitions of content are not usually as important as defining the procedures whereby one hopes that content might be attained.

3. Emphasise that school ethos/climate is paramount (see Chapter One). It is a major part of the hidden curriculum. Constantly ascertain the state of that ethos and reflect on ways of improving it.

4. Try to establish positions whereby interdependence and self-responsibility are encouraged and not allowed to slip into competition and blind loyalty.

5. Remember that 'all forms of play appear to be essential for the intellectual, imaginative and emotional development of the child and may well be necessary steps to a further stage of development' (Brierley, 1987, p111).

6. Recall (and celebrate the fact that) enjoyment plays an important part in influencing attitudes to study (APU, 1988, p6).

7. Note that children do not necessarily improve their achievement merely through being frequently tested. Agreed criteria for assessment do not of themselves improve either the curriculum or children's achievements. Put simply – weighing the pig is not the same as fattening it, nor does weighing tell you much about the quality of the preceding meals!

8. Emphasise the role of personal choice and ensure that children see the importance of and consequences of certain choices made. As Peters once reminded us, the development of choice-making is something often denied to us, yet is, in many respects, crucial to our moral structure; surely a good education is in part the assisting of enthusiasms and the recognition of their own consequences and disciplines; the creation of the 'self as a passionate chooser' (Peters, 1973).

9. Note that in any school there will be occasional failures for children (and staff). Whilst failure and diminished self-esteem are rarely good motivators, failure is inevitable in any human enterprise, from time to time. The important point to remember is 'that whilst failure is an inevitable process, negative criticism need not be. It is not failure which gives concern but the way we adults react to failure. *The ideal way to react would be to ensure first that the child was not being subjected to a situation which was totally beyond his level of development* (Lawrence, 1987, p72; our italics).

10. Try to establish an organisation which illustrates a management 'style' which registers that attitude change (often necessary in

children, staff *and* parents) comes best from reduced disso-
nances, not conflict, that in particular a happy staff who care for
one another and enjoy their jobs are likely to have a happy,
motivating school (see Chapter Two).

What is school really for?

Such generalisations as those above are broad, yet moderately practical.
They stem in part from the burden of preceding chapters and from the
research. They are the result of speculation and reflection tempered by
observation and experience. There are few real absolutes. Schools, as
units of analysis, are like people – infinitely different; and to generalise
can be at times to trivialise and diminish. This final chapter is intended
to remind us of what has gone before and especially to rehearse first
principles and directions. Such generalisations need detailed refinement,
specific location and complex action plans. In the above form they may
even appear somewhat daunting, reminding one of the great family
house Victorian recipe and household management books which start
particular culinary delights with such phrases as 'dice one large bullock'.
So, mindful that such exhortations and conundrums concerning the purpose of school may be best expressed in the music of parables, we have
included the following story.

The little boy

Once a little boy went to school. He was a little boy and it was a big
school. But, when the little boy found that there was a way he could go
straight to his classroom by walking in from the door outside, he was
happy and the school didn't seem quite so big any more.

One morning, not long after the little boy had been in school, the
teacher said, 'Today we are going to make a picture.' 'Good,' thought
the little boy. He liked making pictures. He could make all kinds. Lions
and tigers, chickens and cows, trains and boats – so he took out his box
of crayons and started to draw with enthusiasm. But the teacher said,
'Wait! It is not time to begin!' And she waited until everyone looked
ready.

'Now,' said the teacher, 'We are going to make flowers.' 'Good,'
thought the little boy. He especially liked making flowers, and he began
to make beautiful orange and blue and pink ones with his crayons. But

the teacher said, 'Wait! I will show you how to make a flower,' and it was red with a green stem. 'There,' said the teacher. 'Now you may begin.'

The little boy looked at the teacher's flower and he looked at his. He liked his better than the teacher's, but didn't like to say so. He simply turned his paper over and began to make a flower like the teacher's – red, with a green stem. On another day, when the little boy had come into the classroom from the outside all by himself, the teacher said, 'Today we shall make something with clay.' 'Good,' thought the little boy. He loved using clay. He could make all sorts of things, and often did at home. Snakes and snowmen, elephants and mice, cars and trucks – and he took his clay and quickly began to pull and pinch it into shape. But the teacher said, 'Wait! It is not time to begin.' And she waited until everyone looked ready. 'Now,' said the teacher, 'We are going to make a dish.' 'Good,' thought the little boy. He liked making dishes and he began to make some which were of different shapes and sizes. Then the teacher said, 'Wait; and I'll show you how to make a proper dish. There! Now you may begin.' The little boy looked at the teacher's dish and he looked at his own. He liked his dishes better than the teacher's, but he didn't like to say so; and he rolled his clay into a fresh ball again and made a dish just like the teacher's – a plain, deep dish.

And pretty soon the little boy had learned to wait and to watch and to make things just like those of the teacher, and very soon he didn't make things of his own any more.

Then it happened. The little boy and his family were obliged to move to another house in another city; and the little boy had to go to another school. This school was even bigger than the previous one. Moreover, there were no doors from the play areas direct into the classroom. The boy had to go up some steps and walk down a long hall before he got to his room. But the first day that he was there the teacher said, 'Today we are going to make a picture.' 'Good,' thought the little boy and waited for the teacher to tell him exactly what to do. The teacher didn't say anything, however. She just walked around the room talking to each child. When she came to the little boy, she said, 'Don't you want to make a picture?' 'Oh yes,' said the little boy, 'What are we going to make?' 'I don't know until you make it,' said the teacher. 'But how shall I make it?' asked the little boy. 'Why, any way you like,' said the teacher. 'And any colour?' asked the little boy. 'Any colour you like,' said the teacher. 'Why, if everyone made the same picture and used the same colours, how would we know which was which and who made what?' 'I don't know,' said the little boy with a sigh – and he began to make a red flower with a green stem.

No doubt this is a very sentimental story. No doubt many have heard such parables before. But the point is apposite. All may recognise that certain things have been systematically removed from that child during his earlier experiences of school. What he underwent could hardly be distinguished by the term 'education'. His sense of personal responsibility, independence and self-reliance were (presumably) gradually eroded. Initiative, curiosity and creativity were stultified. Is that what school is really for? Many people have written about what school is for. Most are aware that its complex mixture of purposes are not necessarily all *educative*. From use of 'busy work' with one group, whilst working with another, from social control to selection, from 'cooling out' to 'keeping children safe off the streets', from 'fellowship' to the creation of 'elites'; all have their place. Yet, throughout decades and across cultures, despite markedly different philosophical orientations, there is a fair consistency in opinions on what makes a school worthwhile and what school is really about at its central core of purposes. The recent South Australian document (Education Department of South Australia, 1988) set out principles for its primary schools which do not seem overly different from the Plowden Report in England some twenty years earlier. The British Columbian reforms clearly espouse a developmental and individually targeted view of appropriate learning (Province of British Columbia, 1990). Recently, the American Division for Early Childhood responded to the USA position statement 'America 2,000' and the latter's first goal which had been widely quoted in the run-up to the presidential election as 'All children will start school ready to learn'. The DEC make the points clearly. 'Schools should be ready to accept and educate all children. *Schooling will succeed or fail, not children.*' It is, perhaps, worth emphasising some of their other points too, since they are addressing the education of children aged three to nine years or so. 'Early educators must be schooled in and encouraged to use a wide variety of developmentally appropriate curricula, materials and procedures to maximise each child's growth and development.

Achieving long-term academic goals does not imply that young children be drilled in English, science and math. These academic goals are best achieved when young children are provided with environments that encourage their eager participation, exploration and curiosity about the world.' (DEC, 1992, p75) Nearly twenty years ago Postman and

Weingartner remarked that an effective school would seem to have the following characteristics:

1. When time and activity structuring were not arbitrary and could be tailored to the different rates, interests and developmental levels of the child; when children had the opportunity for choice and some organisation of their own time.
2. When it didn't make children unhappy.
3. When the children were involved, rather than passive.
4. When activities took place both within and without the school walls.
5. When school brought diversity to the fore, didn't denigrate difference and accepted other successes than the merely cognitive or 'academic' ones.
6. When school valued self-knowledge and emotional growth and evaluated positively rather than negatively.
7. When school has made its values clear and works in partnership with the community.
8. When school is oriented towards the future as well as to the past.

                                    (Adapted from Postman and Weingartner, 1973)

Conclusion

If one looks coolly and carefully at this book as a whole it is apparent that certain themes and terms can recur from time to time. We have focused upon primary practice, and in doing so drawn from research about 'human growth and development', commented upon 'independence', 'responsibility'. We are deeply concerned with relationships among staff and pupils and have been anxious to emphasise that necessary and delicate balance in learning between content and process. We acknowledge that partnership between parents and teachers is especially crucial in the education of our young. Underpinning each chapter is a support for the 'centrality' of the teacher (professionalism), a concern to debate what effective schooling is really about, and an expression of the need for educational leaders who promote that certain quality of reflection necessary if one is to teach well or provide a good school – whatever the National Curriculum.

At the moment, in many Western societies there seems to be some mistrust, or at best some misunderstanding, between the partners who should be involved in the education of the child. Partly, this is due to genuine misunderstandings, partly it may be the fault of politicians (who, by and large, tend to look for the 'quick fix'), partly it is because primary and early childhood teachers are not known for their ability to articulate practices or principles. *All* of us have a responsibility to see that the values of the school are broadly congruent with the 'best' values of the society; and that these are constantly examined and exposed to the public gaze. But these outside exposures should not be determined or initiated by glib political statements. They need to take place in atmospheres which give teachers confidence; and this latter feature has surely been lacking in England for at least a decade or so. Moreover, outside agencies, whether they be industrial concerns, leaders of commerce or media gurus need to support schooling. They cannot on the one hand deplore the poor spelling exhibited by their recruits from schools whilst at the same time pursuing advertising standards which parade 'catchy' misspellings to influence the young. They cannot demand pro-social behaviour, whilst lauding the competition of the market place or remarking that it is 'good for children to fail' (as one ministerial adviser did in 1990). They cannot ask for inventivenes and creativity in their children if they constantly demand return to old-fashioned or outmoded elements of basics.

True professionalism makes difficult demands on teachers, administrators and their colleagues. It would suggest that, whilst teachers must have time and dignity in the community and not merely be seen as 'delivering' someone else's ideas, they must remain educated, thoughtful, vigilant and reflective. They must be articulate, careful and sceptical. As Thomas Paine once remarked, 'The sleep of reason brings forth monsters.' Educational leaders have a mission; they need to know the job through and through, constantly to return to its reality, constantly to recall that their prime job is to provide a service. Schooling is not a factory process. It is about negotiation, understanding, quality and humanity. There is *no education 'business'*, since the 'products' are not inert, but creative, critical elements in the process.

Learning in schools is not static. An educational enterprise – if it is truly educational – is always 'in the building', never complete. To teach is to be aware that the country gets the schools it deserves. If people value education, inquiry, scholarship, creativity – they will get them. Whilst sharing the rhythms of continuity and change – or acknowledging the twin powers of content and process – we need to create value systems in which schools can grow, be valued and held dear.

Berman once said, 'To deal with aspirations, hopes and dilemmas, students (children) need a rich, invigorating and *problematic* curriculum. Such an unmeasured curriculum can help students deal better with the unmeasurable elements of life' (Berman, 1987, p350). The same might be said to apply to teachers and *their* learning. For their curriculum, too, needs dynamic leadership. We hope that this book will provide a contribution towards it.

BIBLIOGRAPHY

Adler, B and Towne, N (1978) *Looking Out, Looking In,* London, Holt, Rinehart and Winston.

Alexander, R, Rose, J and Woodhead, C (1992) *Curriculum Organisation and Classroom Practice in Primary Schools: A Discussion Paper*, DES, London.

Assessment of Performance Unit (APU) (1988) *Attitudes and Gender Differences*, Slough, NFER-Nelson.

Argyris, C (1989) Strategy implementation: An experience in learning, *Organizational Dynamics*, **18/2**.

Bennett, N (1990) Cooperative learning in classrooms: processes and outcomes, The Emanuel Miller Lecture 1990, *Journal of Child Psychology and Psychiatry*, **32**, 4, 581–594.

Bennis, W and Nanus, B (1985) *Leaders*, New York, Harper and Row in Fullan, M (1992) op cit p28.

Berman, L M (1987) Perception, paradox, and passion: curriculum for continuity, *Theory into Practice*, **xxvi** (special issue), 346–352.

Biott, C (1991) *Semi-detached Teachers: Building Support and Advisory Relationships in Classrooms,* London, Falmer Press.

Biott, C and Nias, J (eds) (1991) *Working and Learning Together for Change,* Milton Keynes, Open University Press.

Bloom, D (1988) *What is the Return on the Investment?* Conference Paper, Child Care Action Campaign, 99 Hudson St, New York, NY 10013.

Blenkin, G M and Kelly, A V (1987) *The Primary Curriculum: A Process Approach to Curriculum Planning,* London, Paul Chapman.

Blyth, W A L (1984) *Development, Experience and Curriculum in Primary Education,* London, Croom Helm.

Board of Education (1931) *Report of the Consultative Committee on the Primary School* (Hadow Report) London, HMSO.

Bolam, R (1990) Recent developments in England and Wales, Ch. 8 in Joyce, B (ed) (1990) *Changing School Culture through Staff Development*, Association for Supervision and Curriculum Development, Alexandria, V.A.

Bredekamp, S (ed) (1987) *Developmentally Appropriate Practice in Early Child-hood Programmes Serving Children from Birth through Age 8*, Washington, DC, National Association for the Education of Young Children.

Bredeson, P V (1988) An analysis of the metaphorical perspectives of school principals, in Burdin, J L (ed) (1989) *School Leadership*, London, Sage Publications.

Brierley, J (1987) *Give Me a Child until He is Seven*, Lewes, Sussex, Falmer Press.

Bulman, L (1986) Arranging and chairing meetings, in Marland, M (ed), *School Management Skills,* London, Heinemann.

Burns, R (1982) *Self-Concept Development and Education*, London, Holt, Rinehart and Winston.

Butt, R, Raymond, D, McCue, G and Yamagiski, L (1992) Collaborative auto-biography and the teacher's voice, in Goodson, I (ed) (1992) *Studying Teachers' Lives*, London, Routledge.

CACE (1967) *Children and their Primary Schools* (Plowden Report) vol 1, London, HMSO.

Campbell, R J (1985) *Developing the Primary School Curriculum,* Eastbourne, Holt, Rinehart and Winston.

Carkhuff, R R (1983) *The Art of Helping*, V. Amherst, Massachusetts, Human Resource Development Press.

Carter, K (1992) Creating cases for the development of teacher knowledge, in Russell, T and Munby, H (eds) (1992) *Teachers and Teaching*, London, The Falmer Press.

Clift, P, Nuttall, R and McCormick, R (1987) *Studies in School Self-evaluation,* Basingstoke, Falmer Press.

Coleman, J S et al (1966) *Equality of Educational Opportunity*, Washington, DC, US Govt Printing Office.

Coles, M and Banks, H (1990) *School INSET: English,* Leamington Spa, Scholastic.

Colman, A D and Geller, M H, (eds) (1985) *Group Relations Reader 2*, Washington DC, A.K. Rice Institute.

Commission of European Communities (1980) *Pre-school Education in the European Community* (Ed Series, no 12) European Communities, Brussels.

Connelly, F M and Clandinin, D J (1988) *Teachers as Curriculum Planners: Narratives of Experience,* New York: Teachers College Press.

Crispus (Anon) (1814) On the education of children, in Greven, op cit (1973), pp 98–112.

Day, C (1991) A balancing act, *Managing Schools Today*, November 1991, pp 41–2.

Day, C, Whitaker, P and Johnston, D (1990) *Managing Primary Schools in the 1990s: A Professional Development Approach*, London, Paul Chapman Ltd.

Dearden, K F (1968) *The Philosophy of Primary Education,* New York, Rout-ledge and Kegan Paul.

Department of Education and Science (1981) *The School Curriculum* London, HMSO.

Department of Education and Science (1985) *Curriculum Matters 2: The Curric-ulum from 5 to 16*, London, HMSO.

Department of Education and Science (1987) *The Education School Teachers' Pay and Conditions of Service Order*, p5, HMSO.

Department of Education and Science (1988) *Task Group on Assessment and Testing* (TGAT Report), London, HMSO.

Department of Education and Science (August 1988) *Science for Ages 5–16*, HMSO.

Department of Education and Science (November 1988) *English for Ages 5–16*, HMSO.

Department of Education and Science (1989) *Initial Teacher Training: Approval of Courses* (Circular 24/89), Elizabeth House, London.

Department of Education and Science (1989) *Planning for School Development* (the School Development Plans Project), London, HMSO.

Department of Education and Science (June 1990) *Geography for Ages 5–16*, HMSO.

Department of Education and Science (July 1990) *History for Ages 5–16*, HMSO.

Department of Education and Science (August 1991) *Art for Ages 5–15*, HMSO.

Department of Education and Science (1992) *Curriculum Organisation and Classroom Practice in Primary Schools*, A Discussion Document (Woodhead, C, Alexander, R, Rose, J).

Dewey, J (1963) *Experience and Education*, London, Collier-Macmillan.

Dickson, A (1982) *A Woman in Your Own Right*, London, Quartet Books.

Division for Early Childhood (DEC) (1992) 'DEC Position Statement on Goal One of America 2000', in *Young Children*, Sept, p75.

Dreikurs, R and Cassel, P (1972) *Discipline without Tears*, New York, Hawthorne.

Duignan, P (1987) Leaders as culture builders, *Unicorn*, **13**, No 4, pp208–14.

Duignan, P A and MacPherson, R J S (eds) (1992) *Educative Leadership*, London, The Falmer Press.

Elkind, D (1989) Developmentally appropriate education for 4-year-olds, *Theory into Practice*, **28**, 1, 47–52.

Easen, P (1985) *Making School Centred INSET Work*, London, Croom Helm.

Education Department of South Australia (1988) *Children and Learning in the Primary Years*, Adelaide, EDSA, Publication Branch.

Egan, G (1982) *The Skilled Helper*, Brooks/Cole, Monterey, California.

Eisner, W E and Vallance, E (eds) (1974) *Conflicting Conceptions of Curriculum*, Berkeley, McCutchan.

Entwistle, H (1970) *Child-Centred Education*, London, Methuen.

Ernst, S and Goodison, L (1981) *In Our Own Hands*, London, The Women's Press.

Evers, C W (1992) Ethics and ethical theory in educative leadership: a pragmatic and holistic approach, in Duignan and MacPherson (eds) (1992) op cit.

Fisher, R (1987) *Problem-Solving in Primary Schools*, Oxford, Basil Blackwell.

Fenstermacher, G D and Berliner, D C (1985) Determining the value of staff development, *The Elementary School Journal*, **85**, 3, pp281–314.

Fullan, M (1983) *The Meaning of Educational Change*, Toronto, OISE Press.

Fullan, M (1992) *What's Worth Fighting for in Headship*, Buckingham, Open University Press.

Fullan, M and Hargreaves, A (1992) *What's Worth Fighting For in Your School*, Buckingham, Open University Press.

Fullan, M and Stiegelbauer, S (1991) *The New Meaning of Educational Change*, London, Cassell.

Gordon, T (1974) *Teacher Effectiveness Training*, New York, Wyden.

Gordon, T (1980) *Leader Effectiveness Training*, USA, Bantam Books.

Griffin-Beale, C (ed) (1979) *Christian Schiller: in His Own Words*, London, A & C Black.

Griffiths, M and Tann, S (1991) Ripples in the reflection, in Lomax, P (ed) (1991) *BERA Dialogues*, no 5, pp82–101.

HM Inspectorate (1990) *The Implementation of the National Curriculum in Primary Schools* (a survey of 100 schools), Stanmore, Middx, Department of Education and Science.

Hall, E and Hall, C (1988) *Human Relations in Education*, London, Routledge.

Hall, B P (1992) *The Holographic Organization: Transforming Corporate Culture through Values*, Paper presented to Second World Congress on Action Learning, University of Queensland, Australia 1992.

Hants LEA with Southampton University (1989) *The Primary School Pupil Assessment Project: Topics in Assessment 3*, Southampton University School of Education Assessment and Evaluation Unit.

Hanley, J, Whitla, D, Dean, K, Moo, E and Walter, A (1970) *Curiosity, Competence, Community: Man: a Course of Study, An Evaluation*, Cambridge, Mass, Educational Development Centre Inc.

Hargie, O (ed) (1986) *A Handbook of Communication Skills*, London, Routledge.

Hargreaves, A (1990) Contrived collegiality: a sociological analysis, *International Sociological Association Conference*, Madrid.

Hargreaves, D (1992) The new professionalism: the synthesis of professional and institutional development, *Keynote paper at Fourth International Symposium: Effective Teachers, Effective Schools*, University of New England, NSW, Australia, July 1992.

Harvey, D F and Brown, D R (1988) *An Experiential Approach to Organisational Development*, Prentice-Hall.

Havelock, R G (1973) *The Change Agent's Guide to Innovation in Education*, New Jersey: Educational Technology Publications.

Hodgkinson, C (1983) *The Philosophy of Leadership*, Oxford, Blackwell.

Holly, P, Hopkins, D and Reid, K (1987) *Towards the Effective School*, Oxford, Basil Blackwell.

Holly, P and Southworth, G (1989) *The Developing School*, Lewes, The Falmer Press.

House, E (1974) *The Politics of Educational Innovation*, Berkeley, CA, McCutchan.

Huberman, M (1983) Recipes for busy kitchens, *Knowledge: Creation, Diffusion, Utilization*, **4**, 478–510.

Hunt, D E (1987) *Beginning With Ourselves*, Cambridge, Mass, Brookline Books.

ILEA (1985) *Improving Primary Schools* (Report of the Committee on Primary Education (The 'Thomas Report')) London, ILEA.

James, C (1968) *Young Lives At Stake*, London, Collins.

Jelinek, M, Smircich, L and Hirsch, P (1983) Introduction: A code of many colors, *Administrative Science Quarterly,* **28**, 331–338.

Jersild, A T (1955) *When Teachers Face Themselves*, Teachers College Press, USA.

Joyce, B and Showers, B (1988) *Student Achievement Through Staff Development*, New York, Longman.

Keiffer, G D (1988) *The Strategy of Meetings*, London, Piatkus Press.

Kelly, A V (1986) *Knowledge and Curriculum Planning,* London, Harper and Row.

Kemp, R and Nathan, M (1989) *Middle Management in Schools: A Survival Guide,* Oxford, Basil Blackwell.

Kutnick, P (1990) Relationships in the junior school classroom: generation, identification and approaches to disruption, in Docking, J (ed) (1990) *Education and Alienation in the Junior School,* London, The Falmer Press.

Kirby, E (1981) *Personal Values in Primary Education*, London, Harper and Row.

Lange, A J and Jakubowski, P (1976) *Responsible Assertive Behaviour*, Illinois, Research Press.

Langham, M and Parker, V (1988) *Counselling Skills For Teachers*, Lancaster, Framework Press Educational Publishers.

Lawton, D (1984) Metaphor and the curriculum, in Taylor, W (ed) *Metaphors of Education,* Heinemann Educational Books, London University.

Lawrence, D (1987) *Enhancing Self-Esteem in the Classroom*, London, Paul Chapman Publishing.

Leithwood, K A (1990) The principal's role in teaching development, Ch. 4 in Joyce, B (ed) (1990) *Changing School Culture Through Staff Development.*

Little, A (1981) *Contemporary Issues in Education: Block 4, Educational Standards,* Milton Keynes, Open University Press.

Little, J W (1987) Teachers as colleagues, in Richardson-Koehler V (ed) *Educators' Handbook*, White Plains, Longman.

Little, J W (1988) Assessing the prospects for teacher leadership, in Lieberman, A (ed) (1988) *Building a Professional Culture in Schools*, Columbia, NY, Teachers College Press.

Little, J W (1984) Seductive images and organizational realities in professional development, *Teachers College Record,* **78**, 339–351.

Locke, J (1690) Some thoughts concerning education, in Greven, P J ed (1973) *Child-Rearing Concepts, 1628–1861,* pp18–41, Itasca, Illinois, Peacock Publishers.

Machiavelli (1513) in Harris, A et al (eds) (1979) *Curriculum Innovation,* London, Croom Helm.

Madden, L (1988) Do teachers communicate with their students as if they were dogs? *Language Arts,* **65**, 2, 142–146.

Marshall, J (1990) *Women Managers, Travellers in a Male World*, Chichester, Wiley and Sons.

Mulholland, J (1991) *The Language of Negotiation, A Handbook of Practical Strategies for Improving Communication*, London, Routledge.

NAEYC/NAECS (1991) Guidelines for appropriate curriculum content and assessment in programs serving children ages 3 through 8, *Young Children*, March, 21–38.

NAHT (1992) *Guidance for Members Teacher, Deputy Head and Headteacher Job Descriptions*.

National Curriculum Council (May 1989) *Science Non-statutory Guidance*, York, NCC.

National Curriculum Council (1989) *Curriculum Guidance 1: A Framework for the Primary Curriculum*, York, NCC.

National Curriculum Council (1990) *Curriculum Guidance 3: The Whole Curriculum*, York, NCC.

Nelson-Jones, R (1986) *Human Relationship Skills*, London, Holt, Rinehart and Winston.

Nias, J, Southworth, G and Campbell, P (1992) *Whole School Development in the Primary School*, London, The Falmer Press.

Orr, D (1990) What is Education? From the commencement address at Arkansas College.

Peck, S (1978) *The Road Less Travelled*, London, Rider.

Peters, R S (1973) *Reason and Compassion*, London, Routledge and Kegan Paul.

Peters, T J (1989) *Thriving on Chaos*, London, Pan Books.

Peters, T J and Waterman, R H (1988) *In Search of Excellence*, New York, Harper and Row.

Postman, N and Weingartner, C (1973) *How to Recognise a Good School*, Chicago, Phi Delta Kappa.

Province of British Columbia (1990) *Primary Program: Foundation Document*, Victoria BC, Ministry of Education.

Rakos, R F (1991) *Assertive Behaviour, Theory, Research and Training*, London, Routledge.

Raths, J (1971) Teaching without specific objectives, *Educational Leadership*, April, 714–720.

Reid, I and Stratta, E (1989) *Sex Differences in Britain*, Aldershot, Gower.

Riches, C and Morgan, C (eds) (1989) *Human Resource Management in Education*, Milton Keynes, Open University Press.

Rogers, A (1986) *Teaching Adults*, p74, Milton Keynes, Open University Press.

Rogers, C (1962) Interpersonal relationship: the core of guidance, *Harvard Educational Review*, **32**, No 4, Fall.

Rogers, C (1968) Interpersonal relationships: USA 2000, *Journal of Applied Behavioural Science*, **4**.

Rogers, C (1969) *Freedom to Learn*, Columbus, Ohio, Merrill.

Rogers, C (1978) *On Personal Power*, London, Constable.

Satir, V (1972) *Peoplemaking*, Palo Alto, Science and Behaviour Books.

Schon, D A (1983) *The Reflective Practitioner: How Professionals Think in Action*, New York, Basic Books Inc.

Schon, D A (1987) *Educating the Reflective Practitioner*, San Francisco, Jossey-Bass Inc. Publishers.

Schon, D A (1992) The theory of inquiry: Dewey's legacy to education, *Curriculum Inquiry*, **22**, No 2, Summer 1992, p119–140.

Schools Council (National Board of Employment Education and Training) (1990) *Australia's Teachers: An Agenda for the Next Decade*, Canberra, Australian Govt Publishing Service.

Schools Curriculum Development Committee (1984) *Guidelines for Review and Internal Development in Schools*, York, Longman.

Selleck, R J W (1972) *English Primary Education and the Progressives*, 1914–1939, London, Routledge and Kegan Paul.

Sergiovanni, T and Corbally, J E (1984) *Leadership and Organisational Culture: New Perspectives on Administrative Theory and Practice*, Urbana, University of Illinois Press.

Skilbeck, M (!982) *A Core Curriculum for the Common School*, London, University of London, Institute of Education.

Skilbeck, M (1988) (ed) *Readings in School-based Curriculum Development*, London, Paul Chapman.

Stenhouse, L (1975) *An Introduction to Curriculum Research and Development*, London, Heinemann.

Sullivan, B M (1988) *A Legacy for Learners* (The Royal Commission Report) Victoria, BC, Queen's Printer.

Sullivan, M (1991) Working and learning in other people's classrooms, in Biott, C (ed) *Semi-Detached Teachers,* London, The Falmer Press.

Timm Paul, R. and Peterson Brent, D (1982) and Stevens, Jackson C. *People at Work: Human Relations in Organizations*, St Paul MN, USA, West Publishing Co., p273.

Tuckman, B W (1965) Developmental sequence in small groups, *Psychological Bulletin,* Vol 63, pp384–99.

Warnock, M (1988) *A Common Policy for Education*, Oxford University Press.

Weikart, D (1987) Curriculum quality in early education, in Kagan, S and Zigler E (eds), *Early Schooling: The National Debate.* New Haven, Yale University Press.

Whitehead, A (1932) *The Aims of Education*, London, Williams & Norgate.

Wolfson College (1991) Conference on Higher Education, Wolfson College, Oxford.

INDEX